SCREENING SICKNESS

Also by Ernest Lehman

Farewell Performance
The French Atlantic Affair
North by Northwest
The Comedian
Sweet Smell of Success

SCREENING SICKNESS

And Other Tales of Tinsel Town

by Ernest Lehman

A PERIGEE BOOK

Perigee Books
are published by
G. P. Putnam's Sons
200 Madison Avenue
New York, New York 10016

Most of the material in this book has appeared in slightly
different form in *American Film* magazine.

Library of Congress Cataloging in Publication Data

Lehman, Ernest, date.
    Screening sickness and other tales of Tinsel Town.

    "A Perigee book."
    1. Moving-picture industry—United States—Anecdotes,
facetiae, satire, etc. I. Title.
PN1993.5.U6L43 1982   384'.8'0979494   82-9134
ISBN 0-399-50683-7   AACR2

First Perigee printing, 1982
PRINTED IN THE UNITED STATES OF AMERICA

For Jane, who loved so much to laugh.

Contents

Introduction
by Helman Sterne

I don't know why you would want to read this book. The
author is crazy. I don't mean he goes around raving like a
lunatic or anything like that. It's just that he's unstable, unpredictable, inconsistent, prejudiced, self-serving, cynical,
sneakily hostile, and worst of all, *not to be trusted*. I know
whereof I speak, but you don't have to take my word for it. If
you decide that you have nothing better to do, and you actually read these pieces, you'll see for yourself how his mind
operates.

Watch how, on those rare, rare occasions when he appears
to be praising movies or filmmakers, he's actually kicking the
bejesus out of them and praising them only so that he can
wear that guileless, guiltless "Who, *me?*" look that's always
on his face to protect him from getting beaten up in public.
That's one of his favorite private fantasies, you know—walk-

ing into one of the film community's most expensive, celeb-
rity-haunted restaurants, or into a high-voltage, heavy-with-
clout Hollywood party, and getting physically assaulted by
someone he has insulted with his typewriter.

But as with almost everything else he does, he is self-defeating and self-deluding. His insults are so covert, so carefully papered over with circumlocutions and what passes for
humor, that people don't seem to realize they've been insulted, and as a consequence, he wastes a lot of money going
to expensive restaurants, and spends a fortune fussing over his
wardrobe for those power-laden Hollywood parties, and goes
through endless hours of karate lessons, all for nothing. He's
never even been *shoved*. Probably, he's never even been *read*,
which is worse yet, and only adds to his bitterness.

Why the bitterness?

I'll get to that. First, I want to alert you to a few of his
more slippery moves, so that you can be on the lookout for
them and don't get taken in.

For example, notice how often he manages to drag in ref-
erences to his own pictures, which is perfectly normal, considering that he's been kicking around Hollywood for a
quarter of a century and can't be expected to write about the
secret life of a parking attendant or something. But the point
is, he very shrewdly drags in only his *hits*, the famous ones,
never the flops that he'd like you to believe never even happened. (Watch this next sentence coming up and you'll see
how it's done.) He's a *Sound of Music* dropper, a *West Side
Story* dropper, a *North by Northwest* dropper, a *Who's Afraid
of Virginia Woolf?* dropper. (See? Simple, isn't it?) Nowhere
do you find him dragging in anything like that little number
he wrote *and* produced *and* directed that was named by a
famous Eastern critic and a famous Western gossip columnist
as the worst picture of the year.

Sift through his sentences and see if you can find any

mention whatsoever of how he sweet-talked a superbly gifted superstar into acting and singing her heart out in a role for which she knew (and he knew) she was too young. Wander through his wordage and find me, if you will, his delineation of the scene that took place the night an equally famous male star threatened to punch him out for having fled to the South Seas instead of going on location with his picture. And what about all those film projects he walked off because he couldn't "lick" them, when all they needed was to be *written?*

Bad memory?

Unh-uh. Convenient one.

I love the way, in his pieces, when the phone rings in his office, it's never a trade-paper salesman trying to sell him an ad, or his doctor's nurse telling him the tests were negative, or a Beverly Hills haberdasher reminding him about the overdue bill. No. Who is it? Cary Grant. Or if he's walking out of a restaurant after dinner, is it ever with one of his tieless, sockless, witless friends on his way out of Hamburger Hamlet? Heaven forbid. *He's* leaving La Scala with Mike Nichols, and he's giving Nichols *advice,* yet. (Like maybe you should believe he guides Abigail Van Buren's love life and feeds funnies to Erma Bombeck.) He's forever trading badinage with his betters, bantering with studio heads just as though there were no beach bums in his life, and no beer, only champagne.

How, you might ask yourself, can he face his friends, his family? The answer is, he can't. They know too much about him. They know what a sham all this stuff is. But apparently there are a sufficient number of people who know nothing about him for him almost to get away with it. (Actually, the number of people who know nothing about him is very, very close to being the actual population of this planet, which is one of the things that has driven him up the wall.)

I would have liked to see him, in these pages, remember how he was once described by his producer, John Houseman, who was appalled by his approach to polishing a screenplay: "He is a philistine going at the Hope Diamond with an ax." Or recall the advice given to him publicly by director Billy Wilder, for whom he was insisting on rewriting a scene even as it was being shot: "Get off this stage immediately and go back up to your office where you're *supposed* to be!" Humphrey Bogart put it only slightly differently when he screamed at him, on a movie set crowded with cast and crew and visitors: "Get this City College writer out of here and back to Monogram where he belongs!"

Dissatisfaction. That's the key to his character. That's what underlies everything he writes. That's where the bitterness comes from. He has been dissatisfied ever since the sixth grade in grammar school. As early in life as that, he had developed some rather amazing mathematical skills. His homeroom teacher, a Miss Abrams, had discovered that he could add in his head with incredible speed and accuracy. So she would keep him after school and read off streams of double- and triple-digit numbers as fast as she could (something to do with her work, of course; he no longer remembers what), and the instant she finished reading off the last number, he would triumphantly blurt out the entire sum total, with unfailing correctness.

It would forever be his most shining hour.

Nothing he has ever done since, nothing anyone *else* has done, has ever come out as perfectly as those lightninglike, all-in-the-head additions. But he has never stopped trying for that same perfection in himself, and never stopped looking for it in others, and never stopped being dissatisfied with the results.

He never should have become a screenwriter. And he never should have become an observer of the Hollywood scene. For the problem is, movies do not come out correct. Some come out more correct than others, but there *is* no such thing as the Right Answer, the perfect picture. Filmmakers and film critics don't have correct answers either. All they have are opinions, evaluations, judgments. Neither art nor show business is an exact science. There are no correct answers. He should have stayed with Miss Abrams, where two and two equal four. He would have been much happier.

And we would have been spared these pieces.

Read them if you must.

You won't learn a thing.

Helman Sterne
National Institute of Mental Dysfunction,
Washington, D.C.

Hollywood
Comes of Age

Whatever goes up comes down. For every force there is a counterforce, for every trend, a countertrend. For each swing of the pendulum to the left, there is an equal one to the right. Licentiousness leads to puritanism. Terrorism leads to vigilantism. Recession leads to recovery. Recovery leads to recession. Obsession with youth in the movie industry leads to success. Success leads to failure. Failure leads to obsession with the *aged* in the movie industry. And *that*, very quietly, is what is going on behind the scenes right now, though you won't find anyone to admit it.

If young writers, young directors, and young producers hadn't had their chance to succeed, and after succeeding, hadn't had their chance to fail, we would not be experiencing the present secret drive toward the use of and dependence on senior cinema citizens to bail Hollywood out, a secret that is being so well kept that only rarely, as in the case of George Cukor's directing Jacqueline Bisset and Candice Bergen in *Rich and Famous* when he was eighty-one, did the world get a peek at what is really going on.

It all started so gradually, so subtly, that no one realized what was happening. The first indication, never stated but strongly felt, was the new philosophy that it is not enough to be a young screenwriter or a young producer or a young director or a young *anything*; you also have to know how to go to the bathroom by yourself. Putting it another way (as many studio executives did, privately, to themselves), it is not enough to be inexperienced and unqualified; you also have to know how to fool *some* of the people *some* of the time. The next requirement was, you also have to know how to fool them *entertainingly* enough to get other people to pay to see you do it.

The change came over the industry almost unnoticed. To some in the business, even at this late date, these words may come as a complete surprise. Attention began to be placed first and foremost on the quality of the product rather than on the vital statistics on a filmmaker's ID card. Distributors green-lighting productions began to forget to ask whether the start date would come before or after the producer's high-school graduation. They began to stop *caring*. This apparent laxity in the front office was soon experienced (and applauded) by writers and directors, too. They no longer had to falsify their birth certificates or conceal their long lists of credits in order to get a foot in the door. It began to become *all right* to have previously demonstrated that one was truly a writer or director, rather than an eager aspirant. (Understandably, this led to many cruelties and hardships among the ranks of former agents, stuntmen, boom operators, cinematographers, and film editors, who were forced to go back

to agenting, stunting, booming, lighting, and cutting in order
to earn a livelihood.)

The next indicator of which way the wind was blowing was
the simplification of the terms of new deals being made with
the studios and the large independents. No longer was a director required to be accompanied on the set by a parent or
guardian. Writers' screenplays would now be accepted even
though done on a typewriter. Gone from new contracts was
any mention of the need to use crayon. Producers were
granted new perks more suitable to their changing needs. Bicycle racks on studio lots vanished, to be replaced by assigned
parking spaces large enough to accommodate a Lincoln Mark
IV. There were even spaces for wheelchairs.

The pendulum swung so fast that it went right *by* the middle ground of the middle-aged, the in-betweens in their thirties, forties, and fifties. The boards of directors of the banks
that ran the conglomerates that ran the studios seemed to
arrive at the same conclusions independently of each other: If
the youngsters who had never done anything before were
driving the industry into the ground demonstrating that they
didn't know what the hell they were doing, and probably
never would, why not turn to the oldsters who had spent
their long professional lives proving their skills over and over
again by contributing to the making of hundreds, no, *thousands* of films that still live on in revival houses and retrospectives and, of course, on television screens far into every
night?

Unfortunately, there was a horsefly in the ointment. How
do you lure the old pros away from their orange groves and
ranches and country clubs and cruise ships? How do you
convince an early winner of the Thalberg award that he'd be
happier in an office at Twentieth Century-Fox fighting to get
the budget of a little domestic drama down from twenty-
seven million to nineteen, happier, that is, than lolling about

on the sun deck of the *QE2* on the Caribbean leg of its east-
ward jaunt around the world? What kind of deal can you
make with a screenwriter who has written forty pictures, won
five Oscars, the Laurel Award, and six Writers Guild medal-
lions for Best Screenplay; what kind of terms will lure *him*
away from playing tennis and golf with his grandchildren on
his own court in Bel Air and on his own links in Palm Desert, in order to sit in an office at the Burbank Studios writing
a script the way the vice-president in charge of production
wants him to write it, which would be insufferable enough
even if she *weren't* dating his grandson?

Everyone knows who the great film directors are. They're
the ones who made all those classics you now store in your
cassette collections, those classics that raised the American
motion-picture industry to its preeminence, and made everyone connected with those films, including the directors, so
rich that they bought up half of the San Fernando valley and
a third of Brentwood and a quarter of Beverly Hills and five-
eighths of Santa Barbara. Why would a hallowed, revered,
healthy and wealthy living legend climb off his horse or out
of his golf cart, or give up his houseboat on the Seine or his
villa in Cap Ferrat, just to save a movie studio from a lousy
fourth quarter by spending sixty-eight days on location directing thirty-one Pintos, twelve quarter-panel trucks, and forty-
nine police cars in an Academy Award-winning auto crash?

Thus, quietly, came the new breed of studio executive, the
one who had to be shrewd enough to know how to drag the
experienced, gifted, proven older pros out of their richly deserved lives of pleasure and comfort and happiness, and bring
them, kicking and screaming, into the movie business as it
exists today. But the executive approach has not been an easy
one. It doesn't always work. Not with producers anyway:

"Harry, enough with retirement, make pictures again.
What do you want with that empty, meaningless, predictable

life of yours when I'm offering you a chance to get back in the fray again in an exciting industry filled with challenge and suspense?"

"What challenge, what suspense?" (is the invariable response).

"Anything and everything. . . . Will the deals people make with you be honored, or will somebody welsh? You never had *that* kind of excitement in the old days. Will the picture you've put into rehearsal actually go into production, or into turnaround, and if it *does* get made, will it be released, or shelved, and if it *is* released, will it run, or will it get canceled after one performance? And if it *doesn't* get yanked, will it be the one picture in fifty that does any business, or will it sink without a trace? *That isn't thrilling? That isn't a challenge?* And suppose it goes through the roof and grosses a few hundred million and you've got a big hunk of the profits. Will you ever see a dollar? Don't tell me *that* isn't suspense."

"But I don't need dollars. I got too many of them as it is. Year after year I made all those pictures with a beginning and a middle and an end, and my stars were taller than five-feet-two and they were willing to work for less than four-million-seven and the directors were willing to study the budget and follow the schedule and shoot the script as it was written, so now I got more money than I know what to do with."

"But, Harry, we *need* you."

"Talk to me again in a couple of years. Right now I gotta catch the Concorde, or I'll miss the season at St. Moritz."

It's no easier with the *screenwriters* either:

"What do you want to sit home for all by yourself, eating lunch all by yourself, writing all those novels that nobody reads, just so you can see your name on the New York *Times's* best-seller list, when you could be here at the studio eating lunch in the commissary surrounded by beautiful

women, and scripting all those exciting properties we bought
for over seven million dollars?"

"Those exciting properties you bought for over seven million dollars are my novels that nobody reads."

"Chester, please, come back to us, write movies again.
We'll pay you four times what Bill Goldman gets."

"I have to finish my next four books, inasmuch as I've
already sold the hard- and soft-cover rights for thirteen million dollars."

"But what's the good of writing books if nobody's gonna
read them?"

"That's all right. They'll go see the movie."

"Chester, we *need* you."

"Some other time, huh? Bo Derek and Jessica Lange are
holding the table for me at Ma Maison."

As for the directors, of course *they're impossible:*

"John, look at me, I'm making you an offer and you—"

"Honey, take out these tubes, disconnect the IV, raise the
bed a little, and sit down here where I can reach you."

"John, listen to me, we'll give you . . . John, will you
leave the nurse alone for *one minute* and *listen* to me?"

"Give baby another big wet one right here, that's my
sugarplum."

"We'll give you two hundred percent billing above the title
in all advertising, and five hundred percent above each theater . . .with *skywriting.*"

"Mmmmm, luvya, honey . . ."

"All the screenwriters you want up to one dozen, final cut,
no producer allowed on the set, a hundred percent of the
profits, and you own the negative after one year."

"When does this picture go?"

"June."

"Sorry, we'll be on our honeymoon, won't we, chicken?"

"At *your* age you're gonna get *married?*"

"At my age you expect me to direct?"

"You can phone it in."

"I can't see the dial anymore."

"Well, can we just *say* you directed and put your name on the picture?"

"What good will that do you?"

"The bank won't give us the loan to make the picture unless we use an *old director*, and you're the only one still available."

"Oh, I suddenly feel . . . strange . . . Something's wrong . . . I think I'm slipping . . . I think I'm going . . . Good-bye, honey . . . Good-bye, world . . ."

"John, you haven't given me an answer!"

Frankly, things are so difficult in this newest of the New Hollywoods that I think by the time you read this, they'll be back to using the kiddies again.

Nobody *Tries* to Make a *Bad* Picture

Funny, it's almost fourteen years now since Pauline Kael called me from New York to ask me to sit for a magazine interview. Fourteen years, and I *still* can't forget the tag end of that long-ago conversation. I'm beginning to think that it sticks with me so stubbornly only because I failed to answer adequately a most pertinent, impertinent final question the rumbustious lady flung at me.

Maybe it's high time.

For twenty minutes we had sparred over the long-distance telephone, she trying to persuade me to meet with her when she arrived in California, I trying to make her realize that I had enough troubles in my life without willingly and knowingly aiding the very woman who had been separated from her position as film critic for a national magazine after panning *The Sound of Music* to examine the life and times and work of the very man who had written the screenplay.

"I mean, Miss Kael, don't get me wrong. I'm *flattered* that a film authority of your eminence would want to do a piece about me, but am I being unreasonable in fearing that there is this infinitesimally tiny possibility that an article by you about me just might, I said, just might, turn out to be something not calculated to contribute to my peace of mind, to my present and future happiness, and to what my agent describes as my reputation? If you knew what lengths I go to to avoid unnecessary pain, your heart would go out to me, right over this phone. You would apologize to me merely for having *thought* of the idea. Do you realize, Miss Kael, that you are talking to the kind of person who once burned to ashes in his living room fireplace a newly arrived, unread, unopened copy of *Time* magazine, merely because a friend had called from New York to warn him that the review of *West Side Story* called the picture the '*Ben-Hur* of musicals'?"

"Dear me," she said.

"Would you really want to do anything that might endanger the precarious emotional health of a person who has just finished playing freshman producer to Elizabeth Taylor, and is now being a sophomoric producer to Barbra Streisand? Have you no pity, Miss Kael?"

"Oh my," she said. "I'm so sorry."

"Thank you," I said.

There was a moment of silence. And then Kael spoke again. "Before I say good-bye, could I ask you one question?"

"Certainly," I said.

"Tell me, Mr. Lehman." And her voice hardened ever so slightly. "Why is it that you people in Hollywood don't make better pictures?"

If I hadn't given up smoking back in grammar school, I would have bitten off the end of my cigar and spat it out.

Instead, I coolly replied, "Did it ever occur to you, Miss Kael, that we're doing the best we know how?"

She broke into peals and peals of laughter. "Oh, come *on* now, Mr. Lehman," she exclaimed and, still laughing, hung up.

Why is it that we don't make better pictures?
Good question.
We're doing the best we know how.
Poor answer.

Poor because it doesn't go far enough, it doesn't take into account all the life situations, the personal dramas, the biographical influences that affect the abilities of filmmakers as they go through the act of doing their thing (acting, writing, producing, directing, photographing, editing, set designing, composing, to name but a few). "The best we know how," if you want my opinion, is really the vector sum of pure talent and the forces that push and pull it away from the horizontal X-axis in the direction of the vertical Y-axis. The result is not enhancement, it is diminution.

Film students, moviegoers, and motion-picture critics usually assume that the people who make pictures are totally devoted to exercising their full skills while making pictures and should be judged accordingly. What the judges see and hear and feel up there on that screen is, they assume, a mosaic of best efforts. Here's what they don't know, or if they do know, tend to forget, just as we who make films tend to forget it about ourselves, and evaluate our work without taking into full account "the conditions that prevailed" at the time of creation or adaptation or interpretation or crucial decision making.

By way of illustration, I give you now some real people, but I won't give you their names. There isn't enough Errors and Omissions insurance in the entire state of California to get me to use their names. Besides you'll know who they are anyway.

Take this director whose films are worshiped by film buffs and critics everywhere for their qualities of soft dramatic focus bordering on loose and shapeless confusion, and hated by others for the very same qualities. Rarely do I ever hear anyone, while discussing this director and his work, bring up the pertinent fact that all of his talent is exercised while he is stoned on pot. It is possible, Miss Kael, that his pictures would be better (or worse, who knows?) if he were able to observe the sign: Keep Off the Grass.

Are the reviewers aware of this? I kind of doubt it. Any more than they were aware of why the films of a noted writer and director of romantic comedies seemed to become more and more cynical as the years wore on. *You* try writing and directing romantic comedy with intractable lower back pain, and let's see how long *you* can remain free of cynicism.

These instances aren't offered as alibis, or excuses. They are offered as bits of data, to be fed into any computer, human or otherwise, that is expected to come up with an accurate answer to Pauline Kael's question.

Take marriage (to paraphrase Henny Youngman) . . . please. For every marriage that was made in heaven, I can show you a movie that was made in hell. (I can, but not now. It would take forever.) There is no single factor on this planet, including the presence or absence of talent, that has a more pervasive influence on the destinies of individual motion pictures and on the careers of their makers than the marital and/or sexual and/or romantic fortunes and misfortunes of the people involved.

The pattern is classic. Given a multiplicity of choices, the producer or the director or the star or any other filmmaker will sometimes choose *this* project rather than *that* project only because this one will take them on location away from an unhappy home life, as they say, for a month or three or four. And isn't it better to do this lousy picture than to get a divorce, particularly in a community-property state? It becomes comical, reading the learned treatises afterward on what was faulty with the film, to realize that the film never could have been good under any circumstances, much less having been made by the wrong people for the wrong reasons. The other side of the coin has on its face the picture of a prominent producer-director who was so much in love with his actress wife that, when her movie career foundered, he took her away from the unhappy Hollywood scene to a foreign country. There, just to keep busy, he made a series of films that unexpectedly revived *his* ailing career and made the charming couple wealthy and contented. Now she couldn't care less about acting, which is why, of course, she's a big hit once again.

Not so lucky the two hotshot directors whose abilities you've all been tearing to shreds in the media and at cocktail parties. Even mentioning them anonymously is like flogging a pair of nameless dead horses. Can anyone examine their last few pictures and point out what the hell really went wrong without knowing that they never would have chosen to make these pictures, and certainly not with the actresses they used for the all-important starring roles, if they hadn't become entranced with the ladies first? From studio executives down to stockholders, never has there been so much suffering in the name of love.

A famous suspense film could have been radically better if the male star hadn't insisted that he would do the role only if a certain female of indifferent ability, but divine proportions, were hired to play opposite him. He had always dreamed of having a shot at her. Well, he got his way, with the studio, and with her. And so it is useless to fault the writer and the director on this one when it comes to pass that the only good performances were taking place off camera. And believe me, this is happening every week of every month of every year. You just don't read about it in the movie advertising.

The ads for a famous screen drama of marital strife failed to announce that so-and-so was playing one of the starring roles only because such-and-such, who wanted it so badly he could *taste* the Oscar, had to turn the role down at the last moment due to his conviction that his shaky marriage would fall apart once his wife heard him uttering that dialogue. And it was for another role in the same picture that a now cele-brated actor had to say a reluctant no, because of his gut feeling that his wife would never see him with the same eyes after he played a man whose masculinity had been humbled. Who *said* wives have no power in Hollywood?

And if the ladies spent less gold at Gucci and Giorgio and Hermes and I. Magnin and Le Restaurant, don't you think their producer husbands would find it easier to say no to the films that should never have been made—but how could they say no? And *you* sit there trying to decide whether it was the screenwriter's fault or bad casting or the director being too heavily influenced by Jean-Luc Godard. Ridiculous. A four-thousand-dollar statement for the month of February from Saks Fifth Avenue, that's what did it. The rest is ir-relevant.

Sometimes, it's too *much* money, rather than too little, that dumps sand into the creative machinery. Some pictures turn out very well indeed and make barrels of bucks for all concerned. What follows from that gorgeous experience is an obsession with keeping as much of the newfound riches out of the hands of the Internal Revenue Service as is humanly possible without going to jail, where it is difficult to make pictures, except on the walls. In the distant but easily re-membered past, I worked on a film with a high-incomed gentleman who spoke with words, just like you and me, but thought only in numbers. He had a way of listening to me during script conferences with a calculating look on his face that truly puzzled me. Then one day it dawned on me. He wasn't listening, he was calculating. *I* was concerned about the holes in our story. He was concerned about the holes in his oil and natural-gas fields. *I* wanted to beef up our characters. He wanted to beef up his cattle. To those of you who saw the picture and had difficulty understanding some of its scenes, please don't contact me, contact my colleague's agent, his business manager, and his tax lawyer, because they were the ones he was working closely with during the entire making of the movie.

So there you have it, Miss Kael. Pictures are not made in a vacuum by robots or computers. They are made in the real world by air-breathing humans. With one hand we write our scenes with flair and wit and dramatic tension, we direct our scenes with sensitivity and intelligence, we act them with knowing heads and uninhibited hearts, we produce our dreams and send them out to thrill and excite and cause laughter and tears and to create untold riches for those who finance us, while with our other hand we fight to find love, to hold love, to keep our bodies alive, to solve our children's problems and our parents' problems, to survive the hostilities of our detractors, the jealousies of our friends, the envies of our competitors. We sit at typewriters and stand behind cameras and bare our souls in front of them, and hunch over Moviolas in cutting rooms and wipe our cold damp palms in screening rooms and recording stages, and we squeeze all of this activity in between visits to doctors and dentists and lawyers and psychiatrists and garage mechanics and plumbers and gardeners and accountants and churches and supermarkets and ballet theaters and ball games and beauty parlors and PTA meetings and funeral parlors and secret motels and the bathroom.

That's why we don't make better pictures, Miss Kael. And maybe it's also why we make them as good as we do.

Logan's Run

Marty Logan had always been gifted with foresight, if nothing else. As far back as late adolescence, he had seen the Hollywood graffiti on the wall and had started lying about his age. Pretending to be the youngest employee ever to work in the mail room at the William Morris Agency, he had gone on, in the years that followed, to become the youngest agent ever to make a deal for Chartoff and Winkler at UA; the youngest assistant director ever to tell Jimmy Caan where he could go (Stage 16); the youngest independent producer ever to announce a slate of twenty-three pictures (one of which got made); the youngest writer-director ever to allow his cast to ad-lib the entire script (it won him the Oscar for best original screenplay); and the youngest executive ever to be appointed vice-president in charge of production for Ajax Pictures.

So preoccupied were the denizens of filmland with their own problems, they had little interest in anyone but them-

selves and therefore failed completely to notice that Marty
Logan was not only not growing older, like most persons, he
was *standing still*, or getting *younger* in some cases. By the
time Logan became production chief, there was literally no
one, including Logan, who knew his true age. And when, a
year later, he ascended to the presidency of the motion-picture division of Ajax Pictures, to become, at twenty-four, the
youngest man to hold that title in Hollywood since Monroe
Thalznick, only a certain computer in the social-security offices in Washington, D.C., knew that Logan was actually
sixty-one years of age. And the computer was not talking.

Things went well for Marty Logan. Ajax prospered, and
Logan grew younger. It appeared that things would go on
going well forever. But then came to Hollywood the Year of
the Young, the Age of Acne. That was when Marty Logan
began to have problems.

You would have thought that the first thing to go, in
Marty Logan's case, would have gone in the privacy of his
bedroom. But Logan had been affluent enough to be able to
unload each of his six wives the day they hit twenty, and he
had disposed of hundreds of other lovely young women at the
first hint of his own boredom. And so, in Logan's unique and
very special case, the first thing to go was his serve.

No one, including Logan, thought anything of it that
sunny afternoon at Ray Stark's house when Logan double-
faulted twice while beating Neil Simon, who was between
plays that day. But in the weeks that followed, Marty Logan's
first service began to lose its zip and go markedly downhill;
his second service gradually lost its outside spin and high
bounce; and before long, Logan was being whipped by players he had formerly beaten with ease.

People began to talk.

First there was the item in George Christy's column in the
Hollywood Reporter; then Jody Jacobs' short paragraph in the

Los Angeles *Times*; followed by a devastating remark in *People* magazine. Naturally, Logan was immensely disquieted by the publicity. He knew what it could do to his reputation. Afraid to take a few lessons from Pancho Gonzalez right out in the open, Logan foolishly persisted in showing up at Ray Stark's house every Saturday and began to press a little too hard. Before long, he developed tennis elbow. And all the ice packs and hydrocortisone injections and all the orthopedic surgeons in Beverly Hills could not put him back together again.

Then came the trick knee.

Suddenly Marty Logan was in deep yogurt, and knew it. For this was the Year of the Young, the Age of Acne. He would have to come through with a superhuman effort to restore his youthful image immediately, or all would be lost—the presidency of the motion-picture division of Ajax, his whole career in the film industry.

Forthwith he canceled all film projects in work at the studio and promulgated a fresh new slate of pictures calculated to impress the industry and the media with his youth-oriented vigor and imagination. There would be Brooke Shields as *Anna Karenina*, throwing herself under the wheels of Ricky Schroeder's tricycle. Gary Coleman would make his film debut in a remake of *Showboat*, singing the classic *Young Man River*. There would be *H.I.P.S.*, a film biography of John Travolta, with Cary Guffey, hair dyed black, playing Travolta in his prime, and John Travolta himself playing Travolta as an old man of twenty-five. A writer was signed for *Coalminer's Granddaughter*. Gene Wilder's homage to Mel Brooks, formerly called *T.A.S.T.E.*, was retitled *Blazing Saddle Shoes*. The green light was given to Tatum O'Neal's remake of *Camille*, in which she would die in the end of chicken pox. And also announced were Cheech and Chong's *Up In Soap Bubbles*, Kristy McNichol and Timothy

Hutton in *On Golden Mud Puddle*, and Jodie Foster, Chevy Chase and Silver Springs in a sensitive treatment of youthful homosexual love, *Making Kaka*.

The Wall Street Journal and *Daily Variety* greeted the announcement of Logan's new production schedule with awe-struck enthusiasm, and there was a surge of renewed regard for the Boy Wonder of Ajax. Logan shrewdly stayed off the tennis courts, and wouldn't even *talk* to Ray Stark, and for a short while, all was well again. Then, one night, in a burst of misguided exuberance brought on by a fresh shipment of Geravitol, the twenty-four-year-old hustler, for whom a dance had been named, leaped out onto the floor at Disco 54 and threw his sixty-one-year-old back out, so far out, in fact, that he made *Time*, *Newsweek*, *People*, and *U.S. News & World Report*.

It was back to the two slices.

The board of directors of Ajax could be heard grumbling all the way from New York. Charlie Flugel could be heard talking of flying out to the Coast all the way from Paris, where he had gone to get away from the grumbling of the board. In his magnificent air-conditioned office in California, Marty Logan shivered with fear and self-loathing, in no way warmed or relieved by the heating pad on his back. He knew, with terror, the danger he was in. If they ever discovered the truth about his age, they would turn the Death Squad loose on him, as sure as his name was Marty Lichtenstein.

No amount of hair coloring or cosmetic surgery or steroid injections, no falsification of birth records or tampering with the computers, would save him. The Law stated that if you were in films, television, or the music business, you left when you reached thirty, and if you failed to leave, or lied about your age, you died. Logan had done both, with a vengeance. It was only a matter of time.

He sat there in his office thinking of all the desperate ploys the others had tried, and he shook his head with sadness. Poor Stanley had escaped to the wilds of Seattle, but they would catch up with him eventually. There was no escape. Poor George had used Max Factor's Sta-Dark #4 on his beard, but even now the dreaded Dye Detectors were roaming the hills of San Francisco to search out the gray hairs and destroy him. And then there was poor Otto, in the jungles of Manhattan. A massive camouflage attempt involving four simultaneous hairpieces had failed to conceal Otto from the merciless Infra Red Team.

The more Logan thought about these courageous men, filmmakers to the very end, the more he sensed in his arthritic bones that his plight was hopeless. Oh, sure, he could get his back handled temporarily, and knock out the tennis elbow and the trick knee with a little Percodan laced with Demerol, and sneak in a few lessons from Pancho after midnight on the back court at the club. He could hang out in a different disco every night, wear nothing but blue jeans and bracelets and necklaces and rings, keep his shirt open to the navel, wear shades, smoke pot, snort coke, shack up with an older woman and call her his "lady," give out interviews about his electric trains in the den and the little QE2 in his bathtub and about how he liked to hang out at 31 Flavors with Steve Spoolberg and George Lukats and Marty Scalese and share rough-cut viewings with them after the Jamoca Almond went down, and hope that the press wouldn't notice the slight difference in their names. But who the hell would he succeed in fooling, and for how long?

With a sigh, Logan rose from his desk and walked into his Screaming Room. (Let the others have their Screening Rooms. He knew what he needed.) He walked into the soundproof chamber, closed the thickly padded door, loosened his tie and collar, threw back his head, and let out a Primal Scream that came from the very depths of his soul:

"It's not fair! I'm too young to go! I still know what the kids want! What's the difference how my body is? It's my head that's important! What's a good backhand got to do with turning out big grossers? I do the hustle where it counts, in my office, not on a dance floor! God, the injustice of it all! All the years I spent standing in the lines with them in Westwood Village, listening to their chatter, getting in tune with their likes and dislikes, sitting in darkened theaters with them, enduring the stink of their buttered popcorn! All down the drain now! Turned off before my time! Snuffed out before I even get a chance to see my pictures on HBO! Never again to read the trades and care! Never again to go to a sneak and sweat! Never again to fight the guilds and sneer! Never to close a deal again, or fire a director again, or break a star again! I won't go! I won't go! I won't go, I tell you, I won't go! . . ."

Logan broke down and began to sob. For almost an hour he wept bitter tears. And then finally he was drained. There were no more tears left. He blew his nose, emerged from the Screaming Room, called in his secretary, dictated a letter of resignation, and left the studio. Then he drove to Bel Air, closed down the house, drained the pool, let the air out of the Rolls and the Bentley in the garage, got into his dune buggy, and turned on the motor to make the final ride to the Motion Picture Country Home.

Suddenly he heard the phone ringing inside the house. He went back in and answered it.

"I just heard that you're free, Marty," the familiar voice said. "We can use you, buddy. How about coming aboard?"

"What about my bad back and the tennis elbow and the trick knee?" Logan said. "Suppose they come after me?"

"We'll give you such protection, they won't be able to get near you," the voice assured him. "It's what you've got upstairs that counts. Forget about running. Your scrambling days are over. We'll give you protection like you've never seen before. Come with us, Marty."

"If you really want me, honey," he said.

And that's how Marty Logan became the new backup quarterback for the Los Angeles Rams.

The Hollywood Party

"John, do you have a few moments?"

"I'm reading a script, dear. Can it wait?"

"Anything can wait, but you're *always* reading a script. When are you going to *produce* one, for heaven's sake?"

"As soon as I find one that I think is worth making. I'll be damned if I'm going to sink a year or two of my life into some disaster, just for the sake of producing, just to stop reading scripts. There's got to be a *reason* for making a picture."

"I'm not asking you to produce one *this minute*. All I'm asking is that you put that script down for a few moments and *discuss* something with me."

"As soon as I finish this, OK? I've got only sixty pages to go."

"How long will *that* take?"

"Four minutes at the most."

"You call that *reading?*"

"You call this *writing?*"

"I'll wait."

"OK. I'm finished."

"Was it anything?"

"Nothing. Very derivative. It's called *All That Classical.* Thinly disguised, and *obviously* about Rudolf Nureyev."

"At least there'd be no open-heart surgery in it."

"Worse. The whole third act is a sprained ankle."

"Oh dear. . . . All right, listen, John, I need some input from you. I'm planning a dinner party for next month."

"Really? What's the occasion?"

"The occasion is, we *owe* about four thousand people."

"Good."

"It's *not* good. We can't go on like this, accepting invitations and never reciprocating."

"Why not? We've been doing it for three years. I don't hear anyone complaining."

"Of course you don't. You're an important independent producer. You hire people. You're a buyer of talent. But what do you suppose people are saying behind our backs?"

"They're probably saying, 'Be sure to invite them. He *hires* people.' All right, what is it you want from me, dear?"

"Ideas. Suggestions. Like, for example, is there anyone in particular you'd like me to invite?"

"Yes. Bo Derek."

"Bo Derek? We don't know *her.*"

"I'd like to meet her husband."

"Who else?"

"Victoria Principal."

"We don't know her either."

"I hear her husband is interesting."

"Who else?"

"Suzanne Somers."

"To meet her husband?"

"Right. And don't forget Lauren Hutton."

"She doesn't *have* a husband."

"Who knows? Maybe they're secretly married. Also, put down Farrah Fawcett."

"Isn't she divorced?"

"Those things don't last."

"Any others?"

"Let me think. . . . Cheryl Tiegs, Barbi Benton, Catherine Deneuve, Susan Sarandon, Barbara Bach, Jaclyn Smith, Loni Anderson, Morgan Fairchild, Nastassia Kinski, Lois Chiles, Cheryl Ladd, Kate Jackson, Shelley Hack, Susan Anton, Linda Evans . . ."

"And I suppose you want them all at your table?"

"I think that would make them feel more comfortable, don't you, inasmuch as they won't *know* anyone at the party?"

"Including you."

"And you can spread their husbands and escorts around at the other tables."

"Naturally."

"You know, dear, maybe you better not try another one of those sit-down dinner parties."

"Why not?"

"Well don't you remember what happened the last time, three years ago? You couldn't sit husbands next to their wives. You couldn't sit wives next to their ex-husbands. You couldn't sit husbands next to their ex-wives. You couldn't sit wives and ex-wives of the same husbands together, and you couldn't sit husbands and ex-husbands of the same wives together. . . ."

"Funny. I don't seem to remember that party."

"Of course you don't. You never gave it. You couldn't."

"What am I going to *do*, John?"

"I'll tell you what you're going to do. You're going to give a huge *cocktail party*, for around five hundred people."

"So big? Why?"

"Then we can invite the Rockettes, and the chorus line of the show at the Lido, and I think there are still a few companies of *Oh! Calcutta!* playing around the country. . . ."

"I hope you realize that we'd have to rent a great big tent."

"Aren't we having the house fumigated for termites next month? Why can't we use *that*, and kill two birds with one stone?"

"John, we wouldn't be killing two birds. We'd be killing a few thousand termites and five hundred guests, most of them, I'm beginning to realize, beautiful women."

"Stop smiling, dear."

"I'm not smiling. I'm just thinking . . . should we use our own Spode chinaware, and our own sterling silver, now that you've let the insurance lapse?"

"Absolutely not. With the picture business the way it is, we'd lose every piece in the first hour. Use Abbey Rents for everything."

"What do you mean by everything?"

"I mean rent *everything*, including a house."

"How can we have guests come to a house that isn't even ours?"

"You think Bo Derek or Cheryl Tiegs or the Rockettes will know the difference? They've never *seen* our house. They've never even seen *us*."

"What makes you so sure they'll come?"

"If they don't, we'll get them from Abbey Rents."

"Shall we invite the critics . . . Chuck and Vincent and Pauline and Andrew and Rex and that bunch?"

"Only if they bring their own bodyguards and food tasters."

"John, do you think there's a valet parking service that can handle *five hundred people?*"

"I'll speak to Hef. I think we should use nothing but Playboy bunnies."

"To park cars?"

"Sure. I'll help each one of them personally. It may take a little *longer* that way, but it'll add an imaginative touch to the evening."

"Yes, and I can imagine every touch."

"Which caterer were you planning to use, dear?"

"Either Milton or Rhodessa or Kristine or Katharine or Chasen's, depending on their availability."

"Why not use them all?"

"That would be *so expensive.*"

"What's the difference?"

"Anyway, I'm only a hundred and twelfth on Milton's waiting list, Rhodessa could only give me a right of first refusal with three months' advance notice, and Kristine has me on standby. If nothing works out—"

"No problem. We can fly in Princess Grace's entire staff from Monaco. It would be a breeze for them."

"Do you realize what that would cost, John?"

"What's the difference?"

"All right, if you say so. Shall I make up the rest of the guest list myself?"

"Of course, dear."

"Is it all right if I invite a few *men?*"

"Of course, dear. But don't overdo it. Maybe three or four."

"Hundreds of invitations. I guess I better send Mailgrams."

"That's not very *personal,* dear. I hate impersonal invitations, and so do you."

"What do you suggest, John?"

"I'll have my secretary hire a special secretary to *personally* call the secretary of each guest. You can't beat *that* for intimacy."

"They don't call you Warm John for nothing, do they, John?"

"Thank you, dear. Now, what about bartenders and all the liquor arrangements?"

"I thought I'd let Jack or Roy or Jim handle everything, with as many assistants as they need."

"Why not get Jack *and* Roy *and* Jim? And just to be on the safe side, I'll ask the president if I can hire the White House bartending staff and fly them in for the evening. They're hardly being used anyway."

"Won't that be terribly costly?"

"What's the difference?"

"Very well. Do you have any preferences in the way of food? The usual shrimp and lobster and cold meats and canapés?"

"If you don't mind my saying so, dear, that's so cliché. Let me call Claude Terrail in Paris and ask him to close Tour d'Argent for a few days. I'll charter a couple of 747s, and the whole staff can fly over with everything all prepared and ready to be served."

"My *God*, John, the *expense*."

"What's the difference?"

"All right. Now, John, you know I don't read the trade papers or the gossip magazines, so you'll have to clue me. Are there any people in our crowd I *shouldn't* invite because they hate each other?"

"Plenty. But with five hundred guests milling about, they certainly ought to be nimble enough and clever enough to be able to avoid each other. *However*, be *sure* not to invite Lester Kerman."

"Why? Even *I* know his picture is on its way to outgrossing *Raiders*."

"That's *why*. There's no way he can avoid *four hundred and ninety-nine people*."

"How about dancing, John?"

"*Now*, while I'm in the middle of reading scripts?"

"No. I mean at the *party*. Shouldn't we have music?"

"Well of course."

"I hope Armando and the trio aren't booked."

"Who needs them? We'll get Count Basie and the boys, and Ella, of course, and we'll spell the Count with Johnny Williams and the Boston Pops, and use Oscar Peterson for background music for those who would rather talk than dance. And I'll get Tigerman Joe to deejay the stuff for the disco crowd."

"John, how in the world are we going to *pay* for all this?"

"What are you talking about? We're not going to pay for *any* of it. The whole party is going to be charged to the picture."

"*What* picture?"

"*All That Classical.*"

"But I thought you said it was *nothing*, that it was *very derivative*. I thought you said the whole third act is a *sprained ankle*. You said there's got to be a *reason* for making a picture."

"There is *now*."

Agent Dearest

Why do I write this memoir? Why add my loving words to all the tributes that have been paid to Stu Magnin? The world already knows full well what a kind, loving, tender, thoughtful, humane, dedicated, selfless person, what a remarkable agent, Stu Magnin is. Will I be able to contribute anything new to the legend? I think so. I do hope so. As a longtime client, I feel I know him in ways that are unique to me alone. It would be a shirking of responsibility, a denial of my affection and admiration for him, were I to hold back now and refuse to share my intimate knowledge with all of you. Stu Magnin deserves total illumination. Stu Magnin deserves to be revealed.

I am constantly asked why I have always addressed him and referred to him as "Mommie dearest." The obvious answer would be: because he insisted on it, to the extent of having it written into my agency agreement. But that would hardly be the whole story. For in my heart of hearts, with my crushed fingers crossed behind my welted back, I have always believed that my calling him "Mommie dearest" was *my* secret way of expressing my true feelings about the man, my way of saying: Stu Magnin is a mother.

His success has always bred envy, and the envious will, I am sure, now seek to read vilification into my words, where only admiration is intended. To these irrational few I want to make it clear that my decision to write this memoir, to reveal the somewhat startling details of my life with Stu Magnin, has no more to do with paying him back for all he has done for me over the years than it has to do with the $400,000 advance Doubledome has given me for the hardcover rights. Considering the enormity of his effect on my life, it would be foolish of me to try to get even. It would be like trying to grow as tall as Mount Everest. And as for caring about the $400,000, I told Doubledome they could *keep* the money, and in fact I refused to *accept* it, until they sweetened the paperback deal to a seventy-thirty split.

No, I feel that in a democratic society the public has a right to know those whom it reveres. Stu Magnin is a public figure regarded by many as being of enormous dimension. "My God, he must be fat!" they say in awe. It is the public's right to *know* that figure, to know the true shape of the body hidden beneath the caftan and the floor-length mink coat. If Blackglama becomes a Legend most, the Legend owes the world a peek under the hem. And if modesty forbids, it is the biographer's duty to lay his subject bare.

All of which is to say that Stu Magnin is not really fat, he is thin. That's right, *thin*. Skinny, in fact, sticklike, skeletal, fleshless, bony, a shadowy wisp of a person bravely pretending on behalf of his clients, through shrewd muumuus and flowing capes and miles of sable, and through artful publicity campaigns loudly trumpeting his desperate crash diets and his desperate craving for caviar and souvlaki and Rocky Road ice cream, through such devices cleverly deceiving the producers and studio heads he deals with into believing that they are hondling with a man of substance.

"That Magnin," they say. "A real heavyweight."

I chuckle when I think of the deception. The grand illusion indeed. Stu Magnin is so thin that he slips through every loophole in our existing tax laws. Once Basil Rathbone, then a client, tried to fire Magnin because he felt it was a case of the thin leading the thin. But he couldn't *find* Magnin to fire him. He was hiding behind John Carradine at the time. So Rathbone wrote a letter of dismissal and slipped it into the mailbox. Whereupon Stu Magnin promptly slipped into the same mailbox through the same slot and disposed of the letter. As one of his greatest admirers once said of him: "No matter how thin you slice him, he's still baloney."

I'd like to add my own observation to that one: Outside of every thin man, there's a fat man crying to get in.

When I was a young client, needing and demanding all of his love and support and protection, Stu Magnin had to draw upon all of his inner resources in order to treat me with the seeming indifference and callousness that the situation rightfully called for. The outside world, seeing the photograph in the newspapers the morning after, knew only of the smiling young screenwriter (that was me) with one arm around the shoulders of his agent (that was Stu) and with his other hand proudly holding the statuette (that was Oscar) for which I had profusely thanked "my agent, Stu Magnin, my own, my very own Mommie dearest, who was responsible for it all." If only I had had more time. I could have told the members of the Academy and the vast television audience how Magnin had broken into my bedroom the night before, had torn the bedcovers from my sleeping form, yanked me out of bed, and thrust a piece of paper into my trembling hand.

"Your acceptance speech," he had snarled, with all the understandable and necessary unpleasantness he could command. "Memorize it, and don't forget it."

"But, Mommie dearest," I had foolishly cried, glancing at the words, "what about the director and the producer and the wonderful cast? What will they *say?*"

"The same as you," he sneered. "I've already written it down for them."

Down through the years malicious tongues have spread false rumors that Stu Magnin often visited physical cruelty and mental torture on his clients. Never has anyone substantiated this evil gossip. Nor has anyone ever been charitable enough, or free enough from personal jealousy, to come forth with an abundance of evidence that everything Stu Magnin ever did to a client was in the client's best interests. I include the following incident in this memoir not because Doubledome insists that I spice things up if I expect to get a whiff of the ten-thousand-dollar bonus for each week I'm number one on the New York *Times*'s best-seller list. No, I recite this illustrative tale only in the hope that it will put an end to the innuendos.

One day quite a few years ago, Stu Magnin took me to lunch on the understandable and considerate pretense of discussing my career, apologizing profusely for taking me to a McDonald's, explaining that Jack in the Box was closed for alterations. Afterward, he asked me to accompany him back to the agency, which I was delighted to do. As everyone knows, Magnin has the only talent agency in the world that headquarters in its own boutique on Rodeo Drive rather than in an office building. The boutique is called No Scruples, and the agents, who are actually salesgirls, are quite striking. There are live film directors in the showcases. Actors can be bought off the rack, and a different screenwriter is drastically slashed every day. Directly underneath the store is a small, bare workroom with nothing in it but a cot, a desk, a chair, a typewriter and a ream of paper, and a heavy lock on the door. In private, Stu Magnin calls this "the rat trap." And it was down into the rat trap that he led me that afternoon.

Pointing to the typewriter and the ream of paper beside it, he said to me: "The studios are looking for musicals. I want one that's good and clean and upbeat, and I want it fast."

"But, Mommie dearest," I protested. "I don't *feel* like writing a musical. I want to make a statement. I want to *say* something."

"Good and clean and upbeat," he said. "A musical. And don't come out until you've written it."

"But, Mommie dearest," I cried.

The door closed in my face, and I heard the heavy lock fall into place. In despair, I sank down at the typewriter and went to work. Three days later, hollow-eyed, unshaven, hungry, and exhausted, I buzzed his secretary and told her to come down and get it.

"Is it good?" she asked me when she had the screenplay in her hands.

"I hope so," I sighed.

"Is it clean?"

"Heavens, yes."

"Is it upbeat?"

"All the way."

"It better be," she said. "He's on the sauce again."

"You mean Perrier water?"

"Yes," she said gloomily. "Straight. Not even a slice of lemon."

"Oh, God." My Mommie dearest was drinking again. Who knew what would happen? I was trembling with fear as I fell into a deep troubled sleep on the cot in the rat trap underlooking Rodeo Drive. In the middle of the night I woke with a scream to see Stu Magnin standing over my bed with my screenplay in his upraised hand, about to strike me in the face for the second time.

"Wait!"

"You call this *clean?*" he shrieked. *Whack.*

"Don't!"

"You call this *good?*" *Whack.*

"Please!"

"You call this *upbeat?*" *Whack.*

"Oh, my head!"

He unbuckled his belt, yanked it out of his trouser loops, and wound up.

"Mommie dearest, don't!" I cried. "That's a Gucci, it could kill me! Look at all the brass!"

"It's gold, you idiot!" And he began to lash me, snarling: "A rock musical? *That's* what you give me—?"

"Yes!"

"About a *whore* who is paroled from a *prison for women* so that she can take care of some *rotten kids* while their father is out *pushing dope—?*"

"Help!"

"And this whore falls in love with the pusher, and the whole damned family forms a singing group called the Seven Roaches, and the big number is called 'Cannabis'? *This* is the way you obey me—?"

"Ow! Ow!"

"Take *this* and *this* and *this* and—"

"Please! Please! I'll clean it up, Mommie dearest! Please! I'll clean it up!"

"Right *now!*" he screamed, foaming at the mouth, his breath reeking of Perrier water. "You will clean it up this *very minute!*"

"Yes, yes, yes," I cried, rushing to the typewriter as he slid the belt back into his trousers. "Just tell me what you want, and I'll do it!"

"You will change the prison to a nunnery—"

"Yes, yes," I said eagerly, pounding the typewriter.

"And the whore to a nun—"

"Yes . . ."

"And the rotten kids to *good* kids—"

"Yes . . ."

"And their father is no pusher—"

"Right . . ."

"He's a baron—"

"A what?"

"Write that down, goddammit!"

"A baron, yes, a baron . . ."

"And he falls in love with the nun—"

"No, I can't!"

"*What?*" He whipped the Gucci out of his trousers again.

"Right! He falls in love with the nun!" I said quickly.

"And they all sing together, the nun and the baron and the kids, but they don't sing 'Cannabis'—"

"Why not?"

"They sing 'Edelweiss.'"

"Edelweiss? Whoever heard of smoking edelweiss?"

He raised the belt over me. "They *sing* it, they don't smoke it!"

He brought the Gucci down hard.

"Ow! Let me—!"

Whack. "And you will not call them the Seven Roaches—"

"Let me out of this trap!"

"You will call them the Trap Family Singers—"

"Yes, yes, the Trapp Family Singers!" I cried, striking the *p* twice in my terror.

"And don't let me hear another word out of you!" he raged. "All I want to hear out of you is the sound of music!"

"Yes, Mommie dearest, I love you, I love you. . . ."

He slammed the door in my face and locked me in the trap again, and in my agony and despair I sat at the typewriter and did his maniacal bidding, heartsick in the knowledge that the world would never see the film that might have been. Had it not been for that strange, hysterical, loving, unpredictable agent of mine, I might have been the proud author of *Snow White and the Seven Roaches*. Instead, it was to be my fate to become known to the world (and now you know how it came about) as the man who wrote *All I Want to Hear Out of You*.

Thank you, Stu Magnin, you Mommie-dearest you.

The Industry

I'm sorry, I think it's time we stopped being so damned defensive about the charges that this is a company town, because (a) it *is*, and (b) our defense is lousy and unconvincing. I've heard the defense (and used it) so many times I know it by heart, and I'm sick of it. Blah blah blah blah blah, it goes something like this:

"Everybody in this town *isn't* in the business, it only seems that way. Just because *we* talk about nothing else doesn't mean *other* people here don't talk about other things. It's no more a company town than, say, Washington, D.C. We've got theaters and museums and parks and a great newspaper, and we've got pro football and pro basketball and big-league baseball and big-time hockey. We read books and newspapers and the national newsweeklies and watch television and go to the movies and the theater and to concerts in order to keep informed, in order to be amused, moved, entertained, distracted, just like other people do all over the country. We talk about Reagan and Begin and Fagin and inflation and the budget and the dollar and the latest mass murder, we talk about *everything* at our dinner parties. We *don't* just talk about the Industry."

Baloney.

Don't you believe a word of it.

It's just a lot of PR we put out because we feel guilty for being so fascinated and excited and stimulated by every aspect of the work we do and, above all, by the awareness that the American people could not very well *do* without, say what you will about it, what we make in this town.

There is no need for apologies, folks. We *are* a company town. Stop denying the truth. There's nothing wrong with it. Face it. Confront it. Admit it. You'll feel better. Frankly, that's what *I* want to do right now. I want to look at a few truths about us, as I see them, and perhaps free myself of the compulsion to adopt the customary Defensive Stance:

We like to hang together with our own kind. At cocktail parties and dinner parties, the husbands tend to cluster on one side, the wives on another, and the men will tend to talk business and the women will tend to talk fashion, and inevitably, when larger talk dwindles down to small talk, the gossip will be about people in the *business. Always.* Because, statistically, there won't be anyone there who isn't *in* the business.

People who are not in the business are called, in this town, civilians. I'm not telling you anything new. I'm just putting it in print, that's all. We *put up* with civilians. We respect them. We'd just rather not be caught at a dinner table between two of them, or pinned down in a corner by three of them. They'd be bored by what we like to talk about, *must* talk about.

The Industry.

Oh, we use a fair share of creative and aesthetic jargon

when we talk and talk and talk about the product, but we are so irremediably, hopelessly competitive in our heart of hearts (which is made of steel or aluminum, not gold) that we impress our critics as being interested solely in money, in winners and losers, rather than in quality. Which is why we get kicked around by the press *and* the public, why we have become, down through the years, synonymous with all that is crass and vulgar in American life.

And when we're not talking about profits and losses, we are whispering (sometimes across the room) about who is shaky and who is in solid, who is about to go and who is about to replace him. In this town, it is not enough for a company to have a winner. Everyone else in the business has to fall on his ass.

Ah, but what about the weather here?

What *about* the weather? What has *it* got to do with our work, or the results? If you can't stand the weather, stay out of the kitchen. Or words to that effect. More accurately, what has the weather got to do with the undeniable fact that those of us who make the big decisions in this town work *indoors*, not outdoors? And what we do indoors is what this industry has been doing for well over a half a century—trying to figure out, on the basis of what the public went for *this* year, what they'll go for in the two or three years that it takes to get the damned thing made.

A crap shoot, that's what it is, and always has been. And the odds are getting worse every day.

In the old days we could strike out over and over again without losing the whole ball game. Today, the banks are looking down our throats and the government is breathing down our backs, a position that only a contortionist could appreciate, inasmuch as the unions are having us by the necks at the same time. Fortunately, no one has got to our heads yet. Fortunately, because our heads are all we've really got going for us.

Let me tell you another thing we have to put up with, we who strive to survive in this much-maligned community. We have to endure the disgraceful snobbism (I can't think of a better word for it, though some of the less accurate terms that come to mind are ignorance, stupidity, prejudice, reverse chauvinism, anti-Americanism)—during all of our five or six decades we've had to put up with the disgraceful snobbism which proclaims that anything foreign is better.

What is so ridiculous about this homegrown attitude is that the rest of the world, when given a choice, which is not always, seems to prefer the Made in USA stamp on everything from Hollywood movies to hot dogs and Coca-Cola. It is only in *this* country that people tend to regard themselves as automatically endowed with high intelligence and sophistication the moment they advertise to friends and foes that foreign is the way *they* go. If it's Italian or French or British, it is, *by definition*, superior, and they, by definition, are superior for recognizing this. No matter that the Italians make dogs as often as we do; the French have fiascoes we never *hear* about; and the British industry is a faded ghost of what it used to be.

Somewhere along the line, I guess, our critics in the press succeeded in making us feel ashamed of ourselves. They kidded our hyperbolic advertising (while taking our money for running the ads) and subtly influenced the public to believe that what we turn out is somehow indicative of everything that is wrong with America. Apparently we *bought* that viewpoint ourselves.

Aside from all his indisputable achievements, is it possible that we bestowed so much respect on Henry Kissinger because of his foreign accent? Does not a Paris label in her gown make an American woman feel confidently, comfortably, incontrovertibly more chic? Does not the sophisticate making conversation at a fashionable Manhattan cocktail party feel infinitely more secure raving on and on about *Chariots of Fire* or *Mephisto* than he or she would about *Raiders of the Lost Ark* or *Annie?*

Foreign is fantastic. Domestic is dirty. How else can you explain the fact that practically every important executive in this town, and not *just* the executive, the affluent so-called creative person, too, drives a Rolls Royce or a Mercedes or a Jaguar or a BMW, *not* a Chrysler or Cadillac or Lincoln or (heaven forbid!) a Ford or Chevrolet or Buick or Pontiac.

You're going to tell me this doesn't *mean* anything? Well, I'm going to tell *you* that you don't know what you're talking about. And if that sounds offensive, it's only because, as I said before, I've decided that the way to go is on the offense. Defense is out. We've tried it for half a century, and it hasn't made a dent. The sneers and the put-downs are the same today as they were in the twenties and thirties. Only the names of the critics have changed. But the bottom line is this, and it's a beaut: The Industry has not only somehow *survived* the slings and arrows, it has become more watched, more noticed, more talked about than ever before.

I'll make just one more point and then get off. I think we *deserve* the ridiculous salaries we make in this business. I think we *deserve* the stock options and the fat expense accounts and all the perks. I think we deserve everything we can get. Because we're living dangerously in this town. We're putting our lives on the line every day of the year. The stakes are huge, and the strain is enormous. If you don't believe me, come on out here to Detroit and see for yourself.

Exteriors

When Ingevar Broodman announced to the world, after months of almost paranoid secrecy, that the new film he was working on would not have *one single serious moment* in it, there were shudders and cries of alarm from those of us who are concerned with the state of the cinema as art rather than commerce. Though the celebrated Norwegian director has never been noted for his sense of humor, most of us nevertheless clung privately to the hope that his announcement was intended as a *joke*, while we publicly beat our breasts over our typewriters.

Looking back on our attitude coldly and realistically, with no indulgence in the luxury of hindsight, it is clear to me that we displayed a grievous excess of arrogance in our journalistic deportment, and I speak here not just of myself but of my colleagues, too. With deplorable bluntness we were saying to Mr. Broodman: How dare you have the audacity to attempt a comedy? How dare you risk the reputation we have worked so hard to maintain for you by, if you will forgive the truth, Mr. Broodman, overpraising some of your films and never underpraising any of them? We do not take kindly to your cavalier decision to go funny on us and ruin not only *your* act but ours as well. Oh, yes, we were mighty upset with you, sir, for you had never once consulted *us* before deciding to flex your creative muscles and try something different. You were exercising your divine right to change, your God-given freedom to expand and grow, and we were damned mad about it.

Yet, it is not with contrition or with embarrassment or with humble apologies that I begin this report now. Those would be mean and small attitudes of mind for so important an occasion as this one. No, it is with nothing less than boundless joy and grateful pride and sheer elation that I shout forth the happy news that Ingevar Broodman's *Exteriors*, which opened at the Village Theatre yesterday, is by all odds (1,000 to 1) not only the most scintillating, witty, uproarious, gut-busting comedy of the past ten years, but also, wonder of wonders, Broodman's finest film to date, superb in conception, flawless in execution, and dazzling in the sureness of its overwhelming ability to delight and surprise a thankful if somewhat aching-ribbed, funny-bone-shattered audience. Never will so many writers on film be so pleased to have been so wrong.

Exteriors is so deceptively simple that a mere recital of its story line would be an act of unkindness to the richness and texture of its magic. One way of summing up this urbane, sophisticated filmic ode to Oslo is to say that it is Broodman at his autobiographical best, as he tells us with infinite charm and rollicking good humor what it was like to have loved and married and fallen out of bed with and then become close friends and professional co-workers with Bibi Osterman, Eva Anderson, Osa Muhlman, Helga Bemelman, Radi Bissell,

Yvonne Klanger, Wendi Whisselburg, Mimi Hansel, Brigitte Weiss, Heidi Hechtinger, Monica Schnipper, Annie Weiselqvist, Britt Auslander, and Booboo Schlotte.

And, of course, what enhances the reality of this romantic comedy enormously is that Broodman, playing himself as the thinly disguised Ingrit Boredman, was able to secure the services of each of the lovely, talented young ladies to portray the fictional counterparts of themselves. Not the least of Ingevar Broodman's genius as a filmmaker has been his unfailing ability to maintain friendly relations with his women in the present long after breaking off relations with them in the past.

But whereas his *Scenes from a Hanging* was a grim, powerful, dramatic rendition of his stormy alliance with Annie Weiselqvist, and his *Geshreis and Whimpers* delineated the Wendi Whisselburg affair in harrowing terms, *Exteriors* gives us the *flip* side of Broodman's unbroken record and positively dares us to take him seriously.

Nervous audiences, caught in paroxysms of laughter, will no doubt be tense with fearful anticipation of the sudden onset of a "thick, turgid darkness filled with menace." The tears of mirth will roll too slowly down the cheeks at first, not quite trusting their architect, expecting momentarily to be wiped out by the wrenching doom and despair we have all come to expect from Broodman. The unspoken thought: He's *gotta* be setting me up, will come to mind over and over, until finally, after perhaps twenty minutes of *Exteriors'* irrepressible merriment, probably in the scene in which Ingrit Boredman releases the trapdoor that sends the Norwegian customs agents plummeting to their deaths, unspoken doubts will vanish and become total acceptance: *Exteriors* is *not* a put-on. It is meant to be laughed at.

From there on you will have the time of your life, so convulsed with glee at Broodman's outrageously funny lampoon of his celebrated hospital bout with a misdiagnosed gallbladder attack, so possessed of the giggles as each of Ingrit Boredman's women begs and pleads with him not to throw her out into the street, pregnant or not pregnant, that you may not even give a thought to the possibility that the Scandinavian genius is revealing terrible truths about himself and laughing at himself in the process.

Whereas Broodman had been, in a sense, hiding his true persona behind the Freudian symbolism of *Ripe Tomatoes*, and lurking in safety, as it were, behind the extravagant emotionalism of *Through a Windshield Headfirst*, he does not hide any part of himself up his sleeve in *Exteriors*. The very title says it all. Here I am, turned inside out. What I have concealed from you in my previous films, I now push to the surface, where you can examine it all and think what you will of it. I am letting it all hang out, and you can laugh at it if you want to. In fact, you *better* laugh at it. If you don't, I am a dead Norwegian herring.

It took courage for Ingevar Broodman to risk his artistic reputation by going against his creative grain. This was not the clown wanting to play Hamlet. This was Hamlet daring to play Ophelia, and without a bathing suit. Broodman's handling of the climactic sequence in which the fictional Ingrit Boredman decides that he must give up his self-imposed exile in Iran after a failed attempt to get the Ayatollah to play himself in Boredman's musical, *The Magic Firing Squad*, skirts the edge of tragedy by a micromillimeter. That is how close its raucous satire is to the truth about Broodman's own temporary exile in Saint Pierre and Miquelon after the much-publicized run-in with the Norwegian Food and Drug Administration over trumped-up charges that the director had concealed several kilos of bran in a hollowed-out script of the anti-Ugandan film, *The Omelet*.

With *Exteriors*, Broodman takes his place in the pantheon

of those few directors who have dared not to stick to their last and have gotten away with it. Like Nora in *A Doll's House*, he has left home, the secure world of morbidity, psychopathology, and the darker regions of the human spirit, to venture forth into the uncharted waters of one-liners, pratfalls, and stand-up comedy routines. And what is remarkable about Broodman's adventurous talent is that he has not sacrificed one iota of his deepest fears and anxieties in the process, nor his lifelong conviction that earthly existence is nothing but a cruel farce. He has simply shifted gears from the heavily dramatic to the light fantastic and said it all, all over again.

Is not the suicide scene of Alf Tillman in *Exteriors*, in which the despondent, terminally ill accountant struggles hilariously for almost five minutes to open the thirty-fourth-floor office window before deciding to hurl his body *through* the glass pane, is that not merely the comedic equivalent of the famous helicopter-blade decapitation scene in *The Musician?* Broodman is not turning his back on his familiar *weltschmerz*. He is simply using *Exteriors* to demonstrate the ease with which a true artist can express the same hopelessness through laughter.

Cinematographer Gunnar Sunkist's poignant lighting of the doomed customs agents, held in very tight close-ups as their necks snap with a loud thwack at the end of their drolly humorous falls, differs from Broodman's treatment of the bathtub murder in *Gillette Blues* only in style, not in underlying intent, certainly not in what the two scenes say about the director's deepest concerns. In both films, the Norwegian is saying that life's worst offerings, such as violent accidental death, come when you least expect them. In *Exteriors*, however, he makes you feel *good* about the prospect, so much so that you would not be chagrined to discover, too late though it would be, that your seat in the theater was the electric chair, with Broodman's hand already on the switch.

During the director's recent visit to Hollywood to gather material for his next film at such diverse locales as the Comedy Store on Sunset Strip, and the backseat of Don Rickles' Cadillac Seville, this reporter caught up with Mr. Broodman at Nate 'n Al's Delicatessen in Beverly Hills the other Sunday morning and found him a bit weary.

"Yes, I'm afraid I am," he sighed. "I have been spending the past week in the studio audience at the Johnny Carson show, studying Mr. Carson's skill in the use of the spontaneous monologue. How would you call it, odd-lib humor? With my unfamiliarity with the language, I have had much trouble trying to read the idiot cards."

"Does this mean, sir, that you intend to continue making nothing but comedies?"

"No, no, no," he protested vehemently. "I intend to stretch my muscles until I have gone as far as I am able to go. For example, I have in mind to attempt a musical western film with much singing in it. How would you call it, a hoarse opera?"

I laughed dutifully.

"Also, I have not yet tried my hand at a thriller, unless you would categorize schizophrenia and androphobia as being thrilling. . . ."

"Hardly," I said.

"Then, I would like to do something with animation. . . ." He frowned. "If I can manage to find a few actors who still have any of that commodity left."

"Are you forgetting the wonderful women who graced *Exteriors* and so many of your previous masterpieces?"

He glanced at me sharply. "Of course not," he said. "I love every one of them. I love the alimony I pay them. I love the child support and the midnight phone calls and the delicately feminine manner in which they cajole me into using them in film after film after film. They keep me on my creative toes. They reaffirm my philosophy of life and prevent me from slipping back into foolish optimism and bland cheerfulness." His eyes took on a faraway look, almost a gleam, and his voice began to shake with emotion. "Above all that I still hope to do, I look forward to one final production with Bibi and Eva and Osa and Helga and Radi and Yvonne and Wendi and Mimi and Brigitte and Heidi and Monica and Annie and Britt and Booboo. . . ."

"Ah hah, a sort of *Grand Hotel*–type story perhaps?"

"No." He gestured impatiently, seeking the words. "A *sufficient* movie . . . A . . . a *plenty* picture . . . It's . . . it's *enough* film, it's *enough* film. How would you call it?"

I looked at him in horror. "*Snuff* film?"

The Norwegian director smiled. "You said it, I didn't."

Anthropology 101

"Good morning, everyone. You're all looking reasonably bright-eyed and cheerful today. I hope that means you did not find the weekend assignment too demanding. Before we start, are there any of you who might have forgotten to hand in their treatises? . . . Good. All right, how shall we attack today's topic of discussion? Shall we begin at the beginning and go chronologically, or shall we jump in wherever the spirit moves us? I'm open to suggestions. Yes, John . . ."

"Sir, during the past semester you have screened for us roughly a thousand films produced over something like four hundred and fifty years of the recorded cultural history of *Homo sapiens,* and we have studied the lives of the people involved in the making of those films. Do you feel it is logical for us to expect valid conclusions from such a statistically small sampling?"

"Yes, I do, John. However, if, in your research, you have unearthed anything that refutes our conclusions, whatever they turn out to be, I'm sure all of us will welcome the corrections, because we all have a mutual goal—to try to understand the mysterious and somewhat inexplicable attitudes of the subspecies *Filmmakers* toward their art, their fellow artists, and themselves, in the hope that this quest will eventually be as successful as Simon Langhart's finding the key to the disappearance of the dinosaur from the face of the earth through microarcheocryobiomaser readings of the Reko particle. Susan, were you raising your hand or puffing up your hair?"

"Both, Mr. Daegonedies. I was wondering if I might give my subjective reaction to a weekend of delving into this strange, ancient civilization."

"You certainly may, Susan."

"Speaking purely for myself, with no attempt at objectivity, I found myself feeling saddened and depressed as I studied the customs and mores of the epoch. I never thought I could be emotionally affected by words and pictures on crumbling microfilm, and by yellowing, faded computer readouts, and yet I was moved almost to tears. To me it was so evident that the artists and their cohorts, they who first *created* this form of life amelioration and communication which they called 'movies' and 'television,' and then developed the art for more than four centuries, they never derived any real pleasure from their work, never realized the importance to their fellow creatures of what they were doing, and displayed an almost universally self-mocking attitude toward their own existence. I've searched and searched the archives, and I still haven't found anything to make it understandable to me."

"May I speak on that, sir?"

"Go ahead, Harry."

"Susan, I think you've allowed your genetic endowment, your L chromosome, to turn you a little soft in the cerebellum. It's a matter of record—it's all *over* the microfilm and the stored data banks—that this subspecies lived remarkably well, had a standard of living way above the average—"

"You're being trivial, Harry."

"No, I'm not. They lived in beautiful, spacious homes, even the lowliest of them in the cultural hierarchy; they had more than ample monetary exchange while it was still in existence; they drove the finest four-wheel surface vehicles of the era; their medical care was handled by specialists; they traveled to distant parts of the planet during their work and their leisure time; they enjoyed celebrity and notoriety; ate in the most expensive culinary establishments; and were looked up to by their fellow creatures as being somehow special. How can you say they derived no pleasure from their work?"

"I'm afraid I'm going to have to interrupt here. We simply cannot get into a debate today. Your emotional reaction, Susan, is every bit as valid as Harry's rebuttal of your viewpoint. Nevertheless, none of us can argue with history, or with archaeology or paleontology. If it is not a fact, it is certainly a *given*, that *Filmmakers* were a relatively unhappy life form over the centuries *despite* the abundant evidence that their work rewarded them with extravagant creature comforts and ego satisfactions.

"Perhaps we would do best to try to understand them in terms of the fierce competitive struggle that characterized *Homo sapiens*, and many other life forms, during the Pre-Electroparthogenic Age in the evolutionary process. The insights we have today have come down to us through tens of thousands of years of trial and error and challenge and a growing cerebral cortex. Magnoplasticene Man is what he is today, knows what he knows today, only because his brain has evolved to its present state. During that distant speck of time known as the Age of Anxiety, when *Filmmakers* made their brief appearance in the universe, sentient beings were not yet possessed of a brain sufficient to grasp the concept that one's own life was in no way threatened or diminished by another man's success. At that particular stage of evolution, *Homo sapiens* had no way of knowing that prosperity and achievement and fulfillment had no quantitative, finite limits, that there was enough, as it were, for everyone.

"Keeping this in mind—their unborn brain cells, so to speak—you will come closer to understanding the self-destructive, embittering, and ultimately self-defeating practices of this interesting subspecies, with its perverse pleasure in the failure of others. I shouldn't say practices, I should say *drives*, over which they had little control. We have seen how these same drives operated in the earliest days of the so-called animal kingdom. Four-legged creatures in the flora and fauna of ancient jungles hunted each other and killed each other more out of instinct than hunger, and had little control over those instincts. In similar manner, various bearers of the culture among *Homo sapiens* during the Age of Anxiety felt impelled, out of a survival instinct, to exercise hostility and aggression, much of it covert, toward their fellow creators, and were moved to envy, jealousy, and the wish to see harm befall the creative efforts of their own kind.

"This phenomenon was not confined solely to the group known as *Filmmakers*. It was equally prevalent among the culture groups that inscribed their work on sheets of paper with a substance called ink. These were the *Bookwriters*, and they were known to be as inexplicably savage toward one another as the ancient beasts of the jungle. So, too, were the creative artists who communicated their messages through music inscribed on discs and tapes, or with oil paints on canvas. The underlying philosophy of the epoch, first uncovered by Crillon in the planet's Temperate Zone, was: 'It is not enough that you succeed. Your best friend must also fail.'

"In your research, I'm sure most of you have come across examples of the ingenious rationales worked out by the cul-

ture bearers of the species *Homo sapiens* to justify to themselves their own tendencies, drives, and developmental
inadequacies. A favorite among the *Filmmakers* and
Bookwriters was to ascribe different values and differing forms
of cultural behavior to the fact of *geographical location*. A
perfect instance of this was the tendency of those who lived
and worked on the easternmost coast of the landmass then
known as the United States of America to feel superior to
their West Coast counterparts in a locality known as California. The arrogance of the former and the defensive hostility
of the latter locked them both in an unending dance of
death, neither group being aware that their cultural output,
their neurotic behavior, and their competitive drives were, in
the long run, identical. Do I see a hand in the rear? Yes,
young lady . . ."

"Professor, you have been stressing incomplete brain development, with its consequent fallacious thinking, as the
underlying cause of the melancholia that afflicted certain
subspecies of *Homo sapiens*. I would like to suggest another
and, *I* think, far greater contributing factor to the so-called
unhappiness syndrome of the *Filmmakers* and *Bookwriters*,
namely, the existence of *money* in the civilization of the
time. A few moments ago, the gentleman named Harry enu-
merated some of the appurtenances of acquisition that
characterized the bearers of the culture during the 1920 to
2370 epoch, and listed these appurtenances as examples of
fulfillment. I see them in an importantly *different* light. For
it was the very fact that monetary exchange was a necessary
part of living that placed the makers of films and books and
music in the subtle psychological trap from which there was
no escape.

"Their cultural works were, perforce, their primary means
of providing themselves with sufficient exchange to purchase
lives of freedom, comfort, enjoyment, and status. To the ex-

tent that their output failed to earn sufficient moneys, they found their lives becoming diminished. It was inevitable that their creative efforts become subjected to evil pressures. As one decade led to another, and one century moved into the next, the culture bearers were forced more and more to shape their works with a strong emphasis on financial return, particularly as money became less and less able to buy a given quantity or quality of anything, on its way to going out of existence completely. And the more strongly the members of this unfortunate subspecies became oriented toward creating and expressing only those aspects of their personalities that would bring them *money*, the more did the other side of their natures feel robbed and stifled.

"Is it not possible that the culture bearers never even consciously realized the true reasons for the consequent bitterness? Is it not possible *(I* think it is *probable)* that they felt guilty and bewildered over the hostility and envy and destructiveness they manifested, all of it brought on by a trap they were in without even knowing it? You cannot begin to understand the cultural epoch we are dealing with in this room unless you see it as having existed during a time period in earth's history when *Homo sapiens* was paid money for what he did, and spent money for what he needed, and acquired nothing he did not pay for, and owned very little unless he got paid a lot for what he did. Thank you for letting me say all this, professor."

"Thank *you*, young lady. I certainly cannot quarrel with any point you have made. True enlightenment is its own reward, but in this instance, you have the added pleasure of knowing that you have made us wiser than we were when you raised your hand."

"How nice of you."

"In passing, I would like to point out how all of us here today are showing ourselves capable of viewing with kindness and understanding and sympathetic sadness a minor sub-species that existed tens of thousands of years ago. If nothing else, it demonstrates the feelingness and humanity of Magno-plasticene Man, as contrasted with his forebears in the dim aeons of the past. But merely because we have been blessed with *change*, that choicest fruit of evolution, as have all living things since time began, let us not be smug about it. Let us instead remind ourselves of the words of La Roche-foucauld: 'The more things change, the more they change. . . .'"

"Sir?"

"What is it, Harry?"

"It wasn't La Rochefoucauld. It was Professor Edward Harley, in his lecture on *The Ecology of the Cosmos.*"

"That no-talent would rip off his own grandmother, if he could find her."

"Professor Harley is very hot in educational circles right now, sir."

"Yeah? *I* hear the lecture was a total disaster."

"Standing ovation, sir."

"His relatives, no doubt."

"And you got the quotation all wrong."

"You know what, Harry? You're barred from this campus. Don't ever set foot in this university again—until I need you."

"'*Plus ça change, plus c'est la même chose.*'"

"You'll never work in this town again."

"Correct translation: 'The more things change, the more they remain the same.'"

"In two words. . . *im-possible.*"

He Who Gets Hitched

Why is this day different from any other day?

It isn't.

It could just as well have been a day in 1958 when you were doing *North by Northwest* with him, or a typical day in 1979 when you were fiddling around with the one he never got to make, *The Short Night*. It just *happens* to be one of those days in 1975 when you were both trying to dig your way into, or out of, *Family Plot*, before you went off to write the screenplay.

In a Full Shot—Day—you enter the bungalow at Universal that is not a bungalow but a studio within a studio, and the outside world immediately ceases to exist. The ever-smiling Sue looks up from her desk, gives you a cheery good morning, takes your luncheon order, and waves you into the office where he awaits your daily presence. You know that he is there even before you go inside, for you have already picked up the aroma of the Flora de Allone 23 that is the advance man for his act.

He is seated in his favorite red leather chair beside the red leather sofa surrounded by beige and mahogany and brass in the tasteful, soothing, orderly office that never changes, year after year after year. Neither does he, with his famous profile now Full Face to Camera, smiling, hopeful, expectant, hands folded over a navy worsted suit and black tie.

"Good morning, old bean," he murmurs.

"Morning, Hitch."

You sit down on the sofa into a Two Shot, eyes glancing at the brass clock on the lamp table across the room. Two minutes past eleven. Seated there you have the advantage, for you will not have to turn your head conspicuously counterclockwise, as he will so many times during the hours to come, to see how long to go before the earth's rotation finally releases you both from the pleasures and pains of working on the film together—until the next day, and the next day, and the next. . . .

The first forty-five minutes are always warm-up time, during which neither of you would dare commit the gross, unpardonable sin of mentioning the work at hand. There are more attractive matters to be discussed first . . . what dinner parties, if any, have been attended the night before, who was there and said what to whom? . . . or, if not a party, what about the movie that was seen last night and was now to be dissected, or, how about those reviews in the morning trades, weren't they shocking? . . . and let's not forget the morning headlines and the stock market and the president and the secretary of state and Lew Wasserman and the Middle East and the sagging U.S. economy. How much more pleasurable, this sharing of the problems of others, than to have to sit there, sometimes in terribly long silences, trying to devise Hitchcockian methods of extricating fictional characters from

the corners into which you painted them the day before. But
the surreptitious glances across the room, and the frequent
counterclockwise ones, finally produce sufficient guilt and
anxiety to force two reluctant swimmers into the icy pool.
Well, up to their big toes anyway.

You know, I've been mulling over what we discussed yesterday, Hitch, and I think I've come up with something that
may make it work.

He looks at you with hope, or is it pity, and murmurs,
Really?

And you begin to talk, and he watches you, and he listens,
and you watch him carefully, and you continue, and finally
you've said it all. And then he does one of several things. His
face lights up with enthusiasm. Good sign. Or his face re-
mains unchanged. Question mark. Or he says absolutely
nothing about what you have just told him, and talks about
another aspect of the picture. Pocket veto. Or he looks at you
with great sympathy and says, But, Ernie, that's the way they
do it in the *movies*. You are now six feet beneath a red
leather sofa, but that is the very worst he will ever allow to
happen to you. But it is not bad, not bad at all, in the old
Hollywood *or* the new.

And now it is his turn, and he trusts you because he is
venturing a suggestion that is bold and outrageous. And he
knows that you understand the anything-goes rules of this
moviemaking game that the two of you play in this office,
otherwise neither of you would risk the embarrassment. So
you look at him steadily and give him your full attention and
listen to all of his ideas, and when he has finished you re-
spond with one of your own personal devices for dealing with
the sensitive work relationship.

Hey, that's nifty, Hitch. I really *like* that. . . .

Hmmm . . . yes, that has possibilities. . . .

Very interesting . . . really interesting . . . I think we ought to throw it in the hopper with all the others . . . I don't know . . . I see what you mean . . . but I don't know. . . .

The rules—never acknowledged or articulated—are: I won't hurt you if you don't hurt me, provided neither of us lets the other hurt the picture. I'll let you fight me if you let me fight you, provided neither of us forgets that the main fight is to entertain an audience. Don't be ashamed of anything. *Say* it.

And so it goes, back and forth, give a little, take a little, win a few, lose a few, laugh a little, squirm a little, too much talk, too much silence, Hitch doesn't like anything I say, Ernie doesn't like anything I say, the trouble with directors is, they want to go from A to G, and you can't just *go* from A to G, you have to have a reason for going there and a way of getting there . . . the trouble with writers is, they always want to know *why* or *how*, they're so pedestrian. . . .

And always, the real fun is to toy with the ones that got away, maybe to be used in some other flick or maybe never at all . . . Cary Grant, do you know that you were almost killed by a tidal wave that was overtaking your escaping Piper Cub plane as you took off from the frozen tundra of Alaska? (*You* know, Cary, the kind of tidal wave that's caused by the explosion of an atomic warhead on a missile that has been secretly tampered with to make it *reverse* its trajectory and return to its launching pad?) . . . Bruce Dern, you don't know how lucky you are to be alive today after (*a*) being driven in a locked car off a rickety bridge into a deep reservoir and (*b*) being pushed off a platform in front of a speeding Bay Area Rapid Transit train. Yes, if the walls of that quiet, orderly office could speak, they would long ago have pronounced two timid film-makers guilty of having conspired to commit some of the foulest murders ever conceived by man. And it was not the laws of the land that saved the intended victims, but the laws of story construction.

The office door bursts open. It is five seconds past twelve-thirty. The studio waiter is bearing two trays. We stretch our creaking brains and go into the private dining room a few feet away and sit down to New York steak and black coffee. The story problems can go to the devil. This is conversation time, much of it about rare dishes and vintage wines, because there are no calories in small talk, or in flashbacks to the triumphs and the defeats of yesteryear. Both of us know that you can't have the triumphs without the defeats, unless you are lucky enough to get hit by a truck at a very early age. And the indignities, the humiliations . . .

Did I ever tell you what Selznick once did to me? . . .

You think *that's* something, let me tell you about Jack . . .

It's amazing how many awful things other people have done to you if you've had a career in films. You've never done anything to *them.*

And the droll stories . . . if only you could remember them *all.* But what's the difference, you'd never be able to tell them the way he does anyway.

"This actress came up to me while I was shooting *Lifeboat* at Twentieth Century-Fox and said, 'Mr. Hitchcock, is there *nothing* you can do about Tallulah? She refuses to wear panties beneath her skirt, and every time she climbs up into the set . . .' Young woman, I replied, that is not my department. 'Then whose department *is* it?' she cried. I suggest, I explained to her, that you take it up with either makeup or hairdressing."

Writer Chokes to Death on Piece of Steak While Laughing. Of course. The perfect murder. Leave it to him. And you can't blame him, either. You wish you knew one yourself.

Can it be twenty to two, for God's sake? It sure can. Easily.

Shall we return to our toy trains? he inquires, lighting a cigar.

Back to the drawing board—the red leather chair and the red leather sofa—and now it is a race against too little time. Where were we?

I believe we were at the point where the bishop was opening the back door and falling out of the car . . .

But, Hitch, I thought we had agreed that he can't open the back door if he's unconscious . . .

Well, if he doesn't open the back door and fall out, how will she be able to see him? . . .

She won't. So we'll have to come up with another—

But think of the look on her face when she sees the bishop's head fall out of the open back door . . .

How can an unconscious man reach up and open a car door? . . .

I'll shoot her point of view, and the bishop's mouth will be hanging open like this, only upside down, of course . . .

But if he's *unconscious* . . .

Did I ever tell you about the time I ran into Dorothy Hammerstein in a New York restaurant after having not seen her for thirty years? . . .

No, please do . . .

At three-fifteen, the door opens and Sue comes in with two wineglasses of chilled Fresca over a single ice cube. She closes the door after leaving, and you drink and struggle over the bishop until the Fresca is gone. Then he calls out loudly for another glass, this time with two blocks of ice, please. Sue enters with a fresh glass—none for me, thank you—and exits with the empty one, and this time she leaves the door slightly open.

To this day, you have not been able to figure out the signal, if indeed there is one. Is it the words "two blocks"? Is it the mere request for another glass? All you are sure of is that the exit door is open, and you are rising to your feet and saying you've got to get to the typewriter to write, or to your secretary to dictate, or to your doctor for another shot of vitamin B-12, as though that's going to do any good, and you are on your way out.

I think we did very well today, don't you?

Terrific, Hitch. Very encouraging. And tomorrow will be even better.

OK, old bean, see you in the morning.

Driving home on the freeway, you *know* that this is all a game leading nowhere, you *know* it's just talk until you both throw in the towel, you *know* that you're never actually going to write a screenplay for a film called *Family Plot*, and even if you did, you *know* he has no intention of making it. Just as you knew there would never be a *North by Northwest*.

Incidentally, the bishop *does* fall out of the car in the movie.

Mouth hanging open, upside down, of course.

Getting It On

I realize that you're not exactly going to fall over in stunned surprise when I tell you that it's not easy to get a picture on the screen these days. Still, it's a phenomenon worth examining. A producer I know who shall go nameless here (which unfortunately is the way he goes in the better restaurants around town) has gotten so desperate that he is going to go totally, one hundred percent, with Special Effects on his next one. No script, no cast, no director, no locations, no sets, no nothing, just Special Effects. I asked him how he expects to attract audiences into the theaters, and he said *what* audiences, *what* theaters, we're gonna *print* them in. He's calling the movie *Revenge of the Picturemakers*.

Right on, Charley.

To him, and to all like him, I have words of advice: Stop complaining. There has *never* been a time when it was easy to get a picture on the screen. Even in the early magical days of the silents, when *The Squaw Man* was racking up huge grosses at the nickelodeons, film productions were constantly foundering on such catastrophes as a director misplacing his megaphone, or a cameraman spraining his cranking wrist, or an off-camera violinist breaking an A string, or an actor running out of eye blacking. Many an epic budgeted at a stunning four thousand two would have to shut down and go hundreds over when a dust storm would suddenly blow up at the corner of what is now Sunset and Gower. Things were really tough then, believe me.

And they didn't get any easier when *talkies* came in either. Sound was one hell of a problem. Out at Culver City, MGM had to construct special stages so that the actors couldn't hear what L. B. Mayer was saying about Irving Thalberg over in the administration building. In Burbank, engineers struggled with the latest in soundproofing to keep the noise of the Warner brothers shouting at each other from ruining some of Bette Davis' earliest films. It is said (though you can't prove it by me) that Stage 26A had its walls triple-insulated with fiberglass, bales of cotton, and back issues of *Captain Billy's Whiz Bang* after it was discovered that three reels of the original sound track of *The Letter* had been ruined by leakage from Jack Warner's jokes.

These were production problems you seldom read about when you study the scholarly histories of Hollywood's infancy and first childhood. Watching "The Late Late Show" and letting the slick black-and-white footage slip past your beer-glazed eyes, it never occurs to you that there was much more to making a film in those days than just tearing a headline out of the newspaper and finding the right word-man at Lucey's bar, or forcing an actress on suspension to either take the role or lose her limousine or her chauffeur, whichever meant the most to her, or getting some male star out of the bed in his dressing room long enough to read from the blackboard behind the camera. Those were nasty, difficult, cynical times, giving rise to the well-known agent who broke a tooth eating his heart out, and the well-known actor at a well-known studio in the well-known city of Burbank whose suicide note said: "Bury me on the backlot, because that's where they killed me."

Today's filmmaking problems are relatively minuscule by comparison. I heard an independent producer complaining at a dinner party the other night. (An independent producer is a producer about whom it can be said, "What's *he* got to be so independent about?") This man was griping that no matter how terrific was the package he had to offer, he found it next to *impossible* to locate the key vice-presidents in charge of production who could give him yes-or-no decisions. I had heard this from other producers, and from agents, too.

This is to tell them all that it is a problem no more difficult to solve than looking something up in the Yellow Pages, or in a Sears Roebuck catalog. There happens to be a hardcover book on the market now called *Executive Lineage* (by Geoffrey MacBain, Bristol House, $15.95), liberally cross-referenced, totally indexed, which enables you, in a matter of *seconds*, to know whether Irving Blow, for example, is at Filmways *now*, or at the *Ladd* Company now, or has just left *Columbia* and is on his way to *Twentieth*, or is already *at* Twentieth, or *was* at Twentieth and is *leaving* Twentieth, or has already *left* Twentieth (and when) and has arrived at MGM/UA (and when), or *had* been at MGM/UA (and for how long) and is now at *Columbia* (and for how long), before moving over to Universal (and when) or possibly *Paramount* (and why). What's more, the publisher, Bristol House (which is rumored to be taking over Universal), issues supplements updating the book every week.

Now, if turning a few pages and looking up a few names and dates in a *book* is too much work for you independent producers and agents, weakened as you are by years of having had everything including the letters from your kids at college synopsized for you by readers, there is a new telephone service you can subscribe to called Locate-A-Veep. (It's in West Hollywood, and I'm not going to give you the address *or* phone number. *Some* things you can do for yourselves.) Locate-A-Veep, run by a couple of hotshots out of Cal State, Northridge, combines your telephone with a computer and four ex-*Time* and *Newsweek* researchers to provide you with almost instantaneous news of personnel changes at the studios on a twenty-four-hour, around-the-clock basis. (A switch on your phone can protect you, if you so want it, from middle-of-the-night front-office reshuffling. And for sixty percent of the full subscription price—a hefty one, by the way—you can limit your tracer service to *female* vice-presidents only, inasmuch as a good deal of the upwardly mobile action seems to be on the distaff side these days.)

Among the *other* cries of woe one hears from contemporary picturemakers, as they go whining and dining on the Bel Air circuit, is the charge that there's no *studio space* left. Studio space is what producers need in order to go in business and stay in business. Without studio space they have no place to install the desks and the telephones and the typewriters and the secretaries and the chairs and the sofas and the carpeting and the posters and the lithos and the lamps and the tables and the filing cabinets so they can put out the announcements and place the ads and take the meetings and hold the interviews and conduct the negotiations and make the deals and hire the writers and develop the properties and have the story conferences and hire the directors and fire the writers and hire the *new* writers and audition the actors and wrestle with the budgets and map out the marketing and promotion and syndication and presales and pay-television sales and Home Box Office sales and foreign-territory sales and publishing tie-ups and fire the directors and hire *new* directors and make up *new* budgets and make some *more* announcements and set *new* starting dates and do all the countless *other* little things that go into the preparation of pictures that never get made.

I've been floating around the studios lately (the rainy season), keeping my ear to the ground and taking notes on the Dialogues of Discontent that seem to be passing back and forth among the filmmakers, and while my notes aren't all that clear even to me, they *may* give you some idea how *some* producers are thinking these days:

First, you've got to find a Property. A Property is known as a Piece of Material. If it's a good Piece of Material, grab it. If it's a bad piece, be careful, don't step in it. (Which is sometimes called a Step Deal.) Never buy a Piece of Material outright. Always take an Option on it. An Option means you own it for six months or a year, or however long you think it will take you to find out the screenplay can't be licked. In order to take an Option, you need Front Money. Front Money is something you get at a place called the Front Office. They give you the Front Money, and you give them the business. This is called a Development Deal.

Next, you hire a screenwriter. He is called the First Writer. His final script is called But That Was Only the First Draft. At this stage, the production is what is known as Ready To Go. This could mean in any direction. Usually it means Down the Toilet, or Down the Tube, depending on the size of the Piece of Material. Anything too large to go Down the Toilet goes Down the Tube.

Another direction it can go is into what is called Turnaround. Turnaround is what you do constantly, otherwise you get a knife in your back. A knife in your back is called the Final Cut. Some directors get the Final Cut. It is their lot in life to get it. It is called the Back Lot. It is also called Getting Points. *Getting Points* was the original title of

Breaking Away, before it was changed to *Breaking Even*. *Starting Over* was the final title of *Being There*, after a Handshake Deal was made. A Handshake Deal is a verbal agreement where nobody speaks. If the picture doesn't get made, you get your hand back.

All of the above guidance can be thrown out the window if you happen to be a producer who can find himself a Young Director. A Young Director is anyone who has never directed a picture before, or who has never seen daylight before, or both. With a Young Director you can get anything made, and often released, too. Finding Young Directors is not difficult if you know which screening rooms to look in. Being able to see in the dark helps.

There are on the market now special eyeglasses which independent producers use for finding Young Directors in the dark. They are called Infra-Redeyes, and are sold exclusively at the Hillsboro Drugstore on Rodeo Drive, which has been run for the past twenty-eight years by two screenwriters between assignments. Infra-Redeyes were invented by Harry Benson and Sam Hedges, two old film directors.

They should be glad they're alive.

"And the Winner Is . . ."

It's too nerve-racking.

You start writing acceptance speeches in your head the day they announce the nomination.

Who should I thank?

Why should I thank *him?* Why should I thank *her?* The *hell* with them, they should thank *me.* If it hadn't been for *me,* there wouldn't have even been a *picture.* I'll be damned if I'm going to give *them* credit for *anything.* Let them win their *own* Oscars. And if they do, they better thank *me.* They better, or they'll be marked lousy in this town. I'll see to that.

Who should I thank?

Better thank *everybody.* Don't leave *anyone* out. The more people you thank, the better you look. Isn't he marvelous? What humility. What generosity. *Listen* to him. None of that "I-did-it-all-myself" crap. Thank everybody. They'll love

you for it. They'll respect you for it. Remember this: The
Oscar isn't important. Winning isn't everything. It's the
acceptance speech that counts.

God, I'm so pale. I'll look awful on television. Better use
makeup. Makeup? What'll people think? What people? The
people sitting next to you in the theater. They'll see *makeup*
on your face. Look at *him*, they'll say. He's wearing *makeup*.
OK, so I *won't* wear makeup. I'm not going to have people
staring at me all night for one lousy Oscar. I'll go to *Palm
Springs* for a week, that should do it. A week in Palm
Springs. A beautiful tan. I'll look great up there.

But how can I get away for a week? I can't drop everything
just like that. I can't leave everyone high and dry just because
I'm going to win an Oscar. But I'm so pale. What'll I do?
Those lights are deadly. Those cameras are merciless. I can't
go up there looking *sick*. *Look* at him, they'll say. He must be
very ill. I'll buy a sunlamp. In *California*? You're gonna use
a sunlamp in *California*? Well, what *else* can I do? It's the
rainy season. I'll buy an expensive sunlamp and I'll go up
there looking terrific. It's worth it. It's *worth* the five
hundred.

What'll I wear?

What do you *mean*, what'll you wear? You'll wear your
tuxedo, that's what you'll wear. You'll wear the black velvet
jacket and the black worsted trousers and the Turnbull &
Asser shirt and the black velvet tie and the patent-leather
shoes with the silk bows on them. But I wore that *last* year.
So what? Are you supposed to throw a thousand dollars'
worth of evening clothes away every time you wear them?
No, but *I* can't go up there in *old clothes*. What'll people
think?

They won't even *know*. They're too busy worrying about
how *they* look. You think they're gonna say, Look at him,
he's wearing the same thing he wore last year? Yes, that's

exactly what they're gonna say. And they're gonna say he's in trouble. Oscar or no Oscar, *he's* in *trouble*. Who needs *that*? You know this town. No one wants to go *near* anyone who smells like he's in trouble. You'd have to be *crazy* to go up there and *advertise* that you're too broke or too cheap to buy a new tuxedo.

So *buy* one then, and stop all the inner turmoil. You haven't done any work in two weeks now just *thinking* about it.

I *haven't* been thinking about it for two weeks.

Well then what *have* you been thinking about?

I've been thinking about my *car*.

Your *car*? What's wrong with your *car*? It's beautiful. It drives like a dream. It looks brand-new.

Yeah? Well it *isn't* brand-new. It's three years old.

So what?

I can't drive up to the grandstand in front of the theater and have all those cheering people see me step out of a *three-year-old car*.

What do *you* care? Those people are just fans. They're just the *public*. After going to the movies every week, they probably can't afford a *bus* ride. You think they'll know your car is three years old?

You're damn right they will. And so will Rona Barrett when she comes up to me with her microphone. The first thing she'll say to me is, When did you start collecting old cars? *I* know *her*. And when I drive up to the Governors' Ball after the awards, I can see the paparazzi positively *blinding* me with their flashbulbs and climbing all over each other to get a shot of this guy with the sunlamp tan in the old tuxedo getting out of an old car with a brand-new Oscar in his hands, and all the tourists and film buffs and autograph hounds *crushing* the police to get a closer look at this *strange apparition* which is *me*. No sirree, *I'm* gonna hire a chauffeur-driven limousine for the evening. *I* know they're all gone by now, but there's a black-market outfit where you can get one for only seventy-five dollars an hour provided you take it for a minimum of ten hours, and it's *worth* it. It's worth *anything* to feel confident and secure, to *know* that when you pull up in front of the cheering crowds in the bleachers, and Rona Barrett comes up to you with her microphone, the first thing she'll say is, When did you start collecting old limousines?

The table. Who am I gonna have at my table? Why does it have to be *my* table? Why can't I be at someone *else's* table? Why do I have to spend a thousand dollars, or is it *ten* thousand dollars, just because I'm in the Oscar derby? Well, if the nominees and winners didn't buy tables, who *would?* It's your *responsibility. I* didn't ask for this responsibility. *I* didn't ask to be nominated. Well, you *voted* for yourself, didn't you? Yes, but what's *one* vote? Why can't the *studio* heads buy all the tables? They're not *that* busy packing.

You're avoiding the question. *Who* are you going to have at your table? The question is, Who do I want to *be* with? Not my close friends, *that's* for sure. They all voted against me. Acquaintances? Why should I spend a thousand dollars, or is it *ten* thousand, on *them?* How about your enemies? Never. I can't afford that many tables. So *wander* all night. Wander from table to table accepting congratulations from old friends and acquaintances, and no one will ever know that you didn't even have a place to sit.

Oh, yes she will. Rona Barrett will know. The very next morning, she'll ask me, right at the beginning of her broadcast, When did you start collecting old friends and acquaintances?

One thing I know for sure, I'm not going to take a *single ad* in the trades. *Nobody* is going to be able to say I *bought* the Oscar. Not *me.* Sure, everyone *else* will. Especially in my category. It's absolutely disgusting. They'll spend a fortune blowing their own horns, not giving a damn *what* the voters will think of them. *I* know what the voters will think of them. They'll think: *Say*, they must be *good* if they're willing to spend that kind of money on themselves. *Me? I* know what they'll think. They'll think: He must be in trouble, he can't even afford one lousy ad, he'll probably show up at the awards in an old tuxedo and a three-year-old car—*that's* what they'll think. You better take an ad. But how can I word it so it doesn't look like my ad? You could ask a close friend to do it *for* you. A close *who?* The hell with ads. They don't do any good anyway. Your best hope is that your competitors have more close friends than you do.

Suppose I forget my speech?

You haven't even written it yet, how can you forget it?

Well, suppose I finally figure out who to thank and who not to thank and how to say something so goddamn clever that they'll remember the speech long after the picture is forgotten, even longer than Eva Marie's "I may have the baby right here," suppose I do all that and then I go up there and forget the whole thing?

So you'll say thank you and get off, like you should.

Thank you? That's *all? Thank you?* Can you *picture* the seething, burning, bitter resentment that night when they return home from the Governors' Ball and start undoing their ties and corsets and gowns and cummerbunds? Did you hear him? Did you *hear* him? Can you *believe* it? After all I did for him. He doesn't even *mention* me. *Thank* you, he says. The son of a bitch. *I'll get him.*

Don't listen to all this talk about an Oscar boosting your career. Just memorize your acceptance speech or write it on the back of your hand and remember to thank *everybody* because today's propman is tomorrow's chairman of the board, and it won't hurt you a bit if you trip on the stairs

going up to the stage and fall flat on your face because *that*
they'll remember long after they've forgotten your next five
flops.

But it's too nerve-racking.

Thank God I'm not up for anything this year.

Dammit.

I Can Dream, Can't I?

I didn't even have to give it any thought. The idea for the movie came to me just like *that*, while I was showering. It wasn't a *sketchy* notion either. It was all there, the beginning, the middle, and the end. From that, the screenplay flowed like honey, sweet and smooth. Oh, a little first-act trouble perhaps, but the second and third acts wrote themselves, in a mere couple of weeks.

Typing the manuscript, my secretary wept bitter tears during the dramatic sequences. During the comedy scenes, I could hear her from two rooms away, exploding with laughter. "I'm sorry," she said when she was through with the one hundred and fifty-five pages. "I can't take money for this."

"What are you talking about?" I said. "You get two dollars a page."

"I know," she said. "But I had such a good time doing it, I

feel *I* owe *you*. It was an unforgettable experience. Thank you, thank you, thank you."

The next day, I called my agent. But he had just left that morning for a three-week vacation in Mauna Kea.

What the hell, I thought to myself, he deserves it.

An hour later, his secretary called me back. "I thought you'd like to know," she said. "He happened to call in from the islands, and I told him about your script, and he's on his way to the airport right now."

"What for?"

"He's coming right home to handle it."

"But he hasn't even had his vacation."

"You know *him*," she said. "With him, *you're* far more important than a vacation."

He called me the next day from his Beverly Hills office. "Look," he said, "I read the script last night as soon as I got in. You've got big problems, kid."

My heart sank. "I do?"

"Yeah," he said. "You've got until three o'clock this afternoon to decide who you want to sell it to—Laddie, Zanuck/ Brown, Sagittarius, Warners, Paramount, Filmways, MGM/ UA, Twentieth, Chameleon, Columbia, Lorimar, or Universal. They all want it."

"They've read it *already?*"

"*I* read it. That was enough. When I called them and told them how great it was—which isn't easy, because it's that great—they all said yes to the deal immediately, so it's up to you."

"What deal?" I said.

"A million dollars plus eight percent of the gross after double negative."

"My God!" I said.

"All except Chameleon. They want to make a very artistic film. No names, no big directors, no superstars, no exploitation. They're interested only in making a picture that preserves the spirit of your screenplay. Their offer was seventy-five thousand and no points, which is understandable."

I thought it over for a moment. "What's *your* recommendation?" I said to my agent.

"Doesn't it seem obvious?" he replied. "You've *got* to go with Chameleon."

"For seventy-five thousand instead of a million?" I cried.

"Quality, kid, quality. That's all *I'm* interested in."

So I instructed him to close with Sagittarius immediately for a million, which he did, protesting bitterly. When I reminded him of his hundred-thousand-dollar commission, he hung up on me in disgust.

The chairman of the board of Dow Chemical, which owns the company that owns Sagittarius, called me personally to thank me for letting them have the screenplay. He told me that he had instructed the legal department to write into my contract cast and director approval and the right to the final cut, to help ensure a film that would never make me regret my decision.

Next phone call: Who did I want, George Roy Hill, Robert Benton, Bob Wise, Arthur Hiller, Billy Wilder, Alan Pakula, Francis Coppola, Jim Bridges, Marty Ritt, or Herb Ross? They were all so hot to direct the picture, they didn't care *what* their deal was, and they *loved* the idea of my having the final cut. It would help them so much to capture the essence of what I had written.

"Look, I appreciate the call," I said, "but you guys paid the one mil. I think the choice should be yours. And besides, why should *I*, who only *wrote* the film, know more about who's right for it than Dow Chemical?"

They felt I was being a little *too* modest, but they went along with me, and made their own selection, and didn't bother me again until casting time came. Nicholson, Pacino,

Newman, Hoffman, De Niro, Travolta, Redford, Lemmon, Dreyfuss, Scheider, and Reynolds would take any role in the picture, just so long as they were *in* it. Who did I want?

"Gee, they're all so wonderful," I said. "It's so hard to choose."

"Tell you what then," the Dow Chemical guy said. "We'll make it easy for you. You can have them all."

"All?" I cried. "How can the picture afford *that?*"

"Easily," he said. "They've all agreed to take one-eighth of their deals. And I forgot to tell you—if you want Matthau, Hackman, and Beatty to do cameos as the three Mulligan brothers, they're willing to give us a week at scale."

"They'd be perfect," I said.

"You've got them then," he said. "Now, as for the two *feminine* leads, it's almost the same story. They don't care *which* role they play, as long as they're in the picture."

"*Who* doesn't care?"

"Jane Fonda, Barbra Streisand, Faye Dunaway, Bette Midler, Jackie Bisset, Meryl Streep, Sophia Loren, Liza Minnelli, Mariel Hemingway, Julie Andrews, Glenda Jackson, Sissy Spacek, Karen Black, Brooke Shields, Lauren Hutton, and Jill Clayburgh."

My head was spinning. "I can't have them all, can I?"

"We'd love to do that for you," the man said, "but there are only two speaking parts for women in the whole picture."

"Of course. I forgot."

"So pick two then. . . . Go ahead."

"I . . . I just *can't do it,*" I stammered.

"Why not?"

"What'll the others think? What'll they *say?* They'll feel so *rejected.*"

"Tell you what, then. Why don't you write in fourteen additional small women's roles? Think you could do that?"

"That's very kind of you. But it'll take me at least a week."

"Don't worry," he said. "Think nothing of it. We'll pay you an extra twenty-five thousand."

"Oh, you don't have to do that," I said.

"I know we don't," he said. "But we want to."

I have no idea how they managed to do it, but they budgeted the film at only three-million-six on a thirty-nine-day shooting schedule, and brought it in in thirty-six days, two hundred thousand dollars under. During shooting, only four lines of dialogue needed rewriting, and for that the director insisted that I be flown in from the south of France. When I saw the first rough cut, I was so overcome, I wept tears of joy and refused to touch a foot of the film.

"I never felt so grateful to anyone in my whole life," I said to the director.

"It wasn't me," he said. "It was your script."

The picture went out with practically no advertising, at the worst time of the year, and within four weeks grossed $56 million domestic. I think it would have gone on to do at least $200 million in the United States and Canada, and God knows what foreign. I'll never know, because that was when I woke up.

Camelot West

Once upon time, in a land called Hollywood, some 3,300 years after the reign of King Tutankhamen, there lived a young king named Richard, who ruled with fierce benevolence over the Fox of Twentieth Century in the Hills of Beverly. The Fox of Twentieth Century did prosper under King Richard, but did suffer economic hardship, too, in much the same manner and in oscillations of fortune and misfortune much like other kingdoms in the land of Hollywood, such as those of King Jack and King Bob and King Lew. But whether times were good or times were bad, there was something in the air in the Hills of Beverly during the reign of King Richard that made his subjects uniquely fond of the young ruler. That something, it is said, was the sound of laughter. For the young king had made it known, without proclamation or decree, but merely by his own example, that victory was sweeter, defeat more bearable, if a smile lighted the features of Twentieth Centurions from time to time.

But that was in another day, another time, long, long ago. For though the many kingdoms of old do prosper today as in days of yore, particularly the Fox of Twentieth Century under King Marvin the Great, there is little laughter anymore in the land of Hollywood. Wise men do not know the reason why, and it is said that their failure to find the answer will lead to their being replaced someday soon by surrogates from the land of IBM called computers, which, alas, do not know how to laugh at all, or even smile.

This, then, is about that bygone time, long, long ago, when men and women somehow managed to smile through their tears, and laughed all the way to the bank—even if it was to plead for an extension on the loan.

I see it all as having taken place about sixteen years ago—during the spring of '67—but it had started really long before that, as long ago as the first time I ever *met* Dick Zanuck. Because, from the very beginning, it seemed to me that the nature of our friendship, for all the affection there was between us, and still is, was tinted, tainted, taunted by practical jokes. There were large ones, small ones, medium-sized ones, sad ones, funny ones, painful ones, gladdening ones—they ran the gamut. But in one important way, they were always the same. They were always on *me*.

Or so it seemed.

What, you may be asking, has any of this got to do with the world of films and filmmaking? Much more, I think, than will be apparent on the surface. For I have finally come to the conclusion that the true rationale for the practical jokes of that Hollywood era (it *was* an era; it's gone now forever) lay in the fact that, because of the unpredictable, unforgiving nature of the business we were in, our telephones were lighted fuses, our desk chairs were powder kegs, the trade papers were letter bombs, and the corridors that led to our conferences and meetings were minefields, and we could never forget it.

We all felt we had too damned many awesome responsibilities, and we didn't like the anxieties we had to live with because of them, but we couldn't give up those responsibilities because the other words for responsibility were position and power and status and authority and money and success. But who *needs* it; *we* needed it. But who *wants* it; *we* wanted it. So we *had* it and worked our asses off to keep it and got even with each other for the Big Game we were trapped in by *doing* it to each other every now and then in one way or another.

What else could we do?

What, after all, is the head of a studio going to do when his friend, who is writing and producing one of the company's most important pictures (fortunately, the company was also preparing *M*A*S*H*, *Patton*, *Butch Cassidy*, *The French Connection*, and *Planet of the Apes*)—when his friend keeps giving him a bad time with casting problems and budget problems and script problems and every other problem in the book? Can he call him into his office and say, "Look, you son of a bitch, you're making my life miserable, do you understand that? *Miserable!* What did I ever do to deserve week after week after month after year of constant, unending headaches and sleepless nights over one lousy picture? What good is it that I'm the head of this studio, the president of this company, if you can spoil it all for me by giving me this trouble? I don't care *what* it costs us, you're fired!"

He could he do *that*? None of us ever did things like that to each other. He couldn't, and knew it, and didn't. Instead, he stole my brand-new Cadillac Coupe De Ville.

"Hello, is this Mr. Lehman?"

"Yes, who is this?"

"You don't know me, sir. I'm a construction worker on the lot here. Do you own a sort of gold-colored car?"

"Yes, I do."

"A Cadillac?"

"That's right. It's parked right outside my office."

"Not anymore it isn't."

"What are you talking about?"

"I just saw someone driving off the lot with it."

"Hello? . . . Hello? . . . Hello!"

We spent the whole afternoon looking for it, the studio police and I. That wasn't too bad. It could have taken a week. We finally found it in a godforsaken corner of what was left of the backlot, hidden behind the crumbling facade of a make-believe Tudor mansion, along with all the other props. Mine didn't look as real. I never said a word about the incident. Privately, I gave him six points on the scoreboard. I figured he missed the point after touchdown. After all, I *did* get the car back.

I forget *what* I did to him in retaliation—unconsciously, of course. I think maybe what I did to him was I handed in the first-draft screenplay of the movie. It was either that, or else it was my interview in the Sunday *New York Times Magazine* about *The Sound of Music*. Joan Barthel had come to town to do a big one, the lead article in fact, on "How Come That Movie Is the Biggest Hit of All Time?" As bad luck would have it (hers), or good luck would have it (mine), everyone connected with the making of *The Sound of Music* was out of town, except the screenwriter.

The *screenwriter?* Uh-huh.

So Joanie took me to the lounge of the Bel Air Hotel, and because I had a severe upset stomach that day (being a Hollywood producer that day), I ordered a glass of Fernet-Branca, and then another, and another, and another, and another. In case you are lucky enough not to know, Fernet-Branca is a powerful and bitter stimulant that is supposed to be taken only by the teaspoonful. I took it by the *throat*. And I don't recall Joan Barthel doing anything to discourage me. My stomach got fixed fast. My mouth was another story. It never stopped talking. Mostly about *me*, of course. Until the final anecdote, the one with which the lovely lady later decided to conclude her lengthy article.

As I see it now, the stolen Cadillac was no excuse. I would not even have *owned* a Cadillac if Dick Zanuck hadn't invited me to do the screenplay for *The Sound of Music*. So there was no excuse, really, for my telling Joan Barthel that Dick had forced me, one day, to stand on the street and say out loud to him, on command, that *The Sound of Music* was a great picture.

He never mentioned the piece to me, though I knew he had read it. But not long after it came out, I walked into the executive dining room, as was my custom, and sat down at the long table with friends and colleagues to have lunch and share gossip. The little room was unusually crowded this day, it seemed to me, and it also seemed to me that everyone present—about thirty or so—was putting more than the usual attention on me. They were all looking at me, listening to me, waiting for my every word. Well, waiting for *something* anyway.

I was waiting for something, too. I was waiting for the waitress (which was one wait too many). Dick Zanuck, at the head of the table, looked at me with concern. "What's the matter, Ernie?" "Matter? I've been sitting here for over ten minutes, and nobody has even come near me. I've gotta eat lunch and get the hell out of here. I've got a picture to make." (Big deal, big man on campus, huh?) "That's terrible," he said. "Why don't you ring that bell there and bawl the hell out of them?" "What bell?" "There." He pointed. Sure enough, there was a little sterling-silver bell on the table in front of me. I had never seen it before. I picked it up and shook it furiously. All conversation in the room stopped. In no time at all I heard dainty footsteps behind me, smelled lovely perfume, and had the menu thrust into my hands. I stared down at it. "Where have you *been?*" I demanded angrily. "I'm sorry," she said. "You're sorry," I muttered. "What's good today?" "How about me?" she said. "I said, What's good?" "How about *me?*" "Look . . ." I put the menu down hard and turned to face her. But I never *did* manage the full turn because, quite frankly, my face got caught in her naked size 34s. And then my eye got caught in her naked everything else (except for the spike-heeled pumps).

And then she sat down in my lap.

I don't know what they were all laughing and screaming about. What's so funny about a guy who doesn't know where to put his hands or his eyes or his red face or anything else? There they were, laughing and screaming, and there *I* was without any lunch. For at least another forty-five minutes. Or maybe it was an hour.

"Three points," I conceded, the next day.

"What do you mean, three points?"

"A field goal. I'm sorry. That's all it was. A field goal. I enjoyed it too much."

What a stupid thing for me to have said. I could see the gleam of challenge in his eyes immediately.

The telephone call came to my office a few days later, at about 6:30 P.M., which was fifteen minutes earlier than any of us ever went home in those days. (No, work wasn't a religion, it was an attempt to survive.) His voice sounded uncommonly serious. "Could you possibly be in my office tomorrow morning at ten o'clock sharp?" "Yes. Certainly. What's up?" "I want to discuss something with you. Not personal, business. And it's not about the picture, or any pictures. It's very important." "I'll be there at ten." "Thanks, old boy."

I did nothing that night but try to figure out what the meeting would be about. Finally I came to the conclusion that he was going to propose that I branch out into television, write and produce a couple of new series, something like that. So I sat up until three in the morning dreaming up ideas and making notes on them. I don't think I slept well, if at all.

He was waiting behind his desk when I arrived promptly at ten, affable as always, but unsmiling. I could tell there was to be no kidding around, no banter. "Sit down, Ernie." I took the chair facing his desk. He murmured into the intercom. "Hold my calls, please." He shuffled some papers, looked up at me. "I appreciate your coming." "Delighted." "This won't take long. I know you're busy as hell." "No problem." "Listen, before we get started, let me go to the john real fast. OK?" "Of course. Take your time." "I'll be back in a jiffy," he said, and rose from his desk chair and went into the next room, which was a combination den and private dining room with bathroom facilities, too.

Quickly I took out my television-series notes and ran through them again. Then I shoved them back into my pocket and busied myself admiring the decor of the brown-and-beige office, the tasteful pictures on the wall, the luxurious beige carpeting. He had been gone no more than three minutes when I began to hear agonized, bloodcurdling screams from the bathroom. It took me several moments to realize that the screams were his, and that someone was attempting to murder him.

I jumped to my feet, knocking over my chair. What to do without getting myself killed? Who would succeed him? Would the picture be canceled? What would happen to his season tickets to the Dodger games? He was screaming for help now. Where the hell were his secretaries? Were they deaf or something? Suddenly the bathroom door burst open. I froze in horror. He was stumbling toward me with his hands clutching at his eyes to stem the flow of blood that must have been pouring from them. He was groaning horribly.

"Dick, what *is* it?"

He fell at my feet on the beautiful beige carpeting, writhing and groaning and clutching at his eyes. I knelt down and leaned over him, wondering what to do, unable to think clearly in the din of his agony. He was making so much noise, I never even saw it or heard it coming. It sprang at me out of nowhere, fangs bared in a hideous snarl, the attacker, the killer, this vicious, hairy, seven-foot ape-man.

Did *I* scream, or was it that body on the floor, writhing with laughter?

I refuse to recall.

Ten minutes later, as I walked shakily to my office, tearing up my television-series notes and dropping them into a sidewalk trash receptacle, two very strong convictions began to take shape in my mind. One was that *Planet of the Apes*, then in production, was going to be a huge commercial success, because it had just proved to me that it could scare an audience witless. The other was that, come hell or high water, Dick Zanuck would never "get" me again.

As it turned out, I was right about *Planet of the Apes*.

The Star System

"Control tower, this is *Superman III* requesting traffic vicinity of Alpha Centauri. Over."

"*Superman III* from control tower. You have traffic at twenty-seven thousand light-years earthbound, Paramount's *Star Trek II: The Wrath of Khan*, estimating the Marathon lot June 1982. Request position report."

"Control tower, this is *Body Snatchers II*."

"Standby, *Snatchers*. Go ahead, *Superman*."

"Control tower, this is *Star Wars III: Revenge of the Jedi*, requesting clearance."

"Stand by, *Jedi*. *Superman III*, do you read?"

"Control tower, did you call *Battlestar Galactica II*?"

"Negative, *Galactica*."

"Roger, switching to Channel Seven."

"*Superman III*, go ahead with your position report."

"Well, gee, thanks. This is *Superman III*, four parsecs earthwest at 0200, estimating Alpha Centauri 2130. Scattered asteroids, visibility one million. Altimeter 21.93 to the twelfth."

"Roger, *Superman III*. AMPTP advises no change in your flight plan. Theatre Owners of America suggest you avoid *Revenge of the Jedi*, vicinity of Twentieth Century-Fox May 1983."

"Roger."

"Go ahead, *Snatchers*."

"Control tower from *Body Snatchers II*, reporting intermittent malfunctioning of right outboard spores. Maintaining altitude, reducing speed to one-half of good old Sol."

"Advise meaning of good old Sol."

"Speed of light, control tower."

"Roger."

"This is *Star Wars III*. Now look, by George, how long do we—"

"Control tower from *Body Snatchers II*."

"Stand by, *Wars*. Go ahead, *Snatchers*."

"Pilot requests, has *New Yorker* review appeared yet?"

"Negative, *Snatchers*. Magazine advises cannot safely do it again. You'll have to arrive in theatres first."

"Pilot advises just passed through time warp, saw flashes of radical change coming up in careers of several New York film critics."

"Describe change, *Snatchers*."

"Negative, tower, you won't believe it."

"Control tower from *Star Wars III*. Say, whose palm do I have to zap to get the frequency around here?"

"Please explain palm-zap, *Wars III*."

"Grease, grease, grease."

"Control tower to *Wars III*. *Grease II* already in orbit worldwide. Went through ceiling."

"Describe ceiling."

"Unlimited."

"*Good.* Request immediate clearance to land."

"Denied. You are cleared by Twentieth to Sirius. Hold at nine million until further notice."

"Notice? What notice?"

"*New Yorker* review of *Body Snatchers II.*"

"Control tower, this is *Body Snatchers II.* Did you call?"

"Negative, *Snatchers.*"

"Roger. Sorry."

"No harm, no foul."

"Control tower from *Star Trek II: The Wrath of Khan.*"

"Go ahead, *Khan.*"

"Over Arcturus 0225 at three-quarters of a parsec descending, estimating the Pleiades 2240. Weather clear, Trek fast."

"Roger, *Khan.* You are cleared to Taurus. Hold at sixteen million for special effects."

"Sixteen million. Special effects. Onboard radar detects heavy clouds vicinity of earth. Please identify."

"*The Swarm II.* Killer bees, moving fast."

"In what direction, control tower?"

"Heading DTT, *Star Trek II.*"

"Was that DDT?"

"Negative. *DTT.* Down The Toilet."

"This is *Superman III.* Did you say Down The Toilet?"

"Affirmative."

"*Superman III* is requesting immediate figures on *Superman II.*"

"Will comply, *Superman III.*"

"And make it snappy."

"Control tower calling *The Late Great Planet Earth.*"

"Control tower, this is *The Late Great Planet Earth.* Go ahead."

"AFI requests condition report."

"Control tower from *The Late Great Planet Earth.* Advise AFI, all's Welles that ends Welles."

"Roger. You are cleared to Mercury. Your alternate is Mars. Advise present weight."

"Three hundred and ten pounds, but reducing."

"Roger."

"Control tower from *Body Snatchers II*, reporting close encounters at twelve o'clock and three o'clock."

"You are in error, *Snatchers*. The movie goes on at one and four."

"Roger. Sorry."

"*Dah dah dah . . . dah dee dum . . . dah dee dum dum . . . dah dah dah.*"

"Control tower from *Snatchers*, what the hell was that? Muzak?"

"That was the mothership, *Snatchers*, thanking us for the correction."

"Control tower from *Superman III*. Have you got those figures on *Superman II* yet?"

"Negative."

"Control tower from *The Swarm*."

"Go ahead, *Swarm*."

"Previous DTT heading incorrect due to pilot error, sloppy reporting of *Variety*; and sloppy variety of *Reporter*. Correct heading should read GTR."

"GTR. Roger. What is your approximate position, *Swarm*?"

"Number one, of course. Somewhere in the Allen radiation belt."

"Do you mean the Van Allen radiation belt, *Swarm*?"

"Negative."

"Roger."

"Is that you, Corman?"

"Negative."

"Roger."

"*Superman III* from control tower."

"*Superman III.*"

"*The Swarm* advises correct heading is GTR, not DTT. Do you still want *Superman II* figures?"

"Did you say GDR?"

"Negative, *Super III.* GTR. Going Through Roof."

"Where did that correction come from, control tower?"

"The Allen radiation belt."

"In that case, make request for *Superman II* figures urgent."

"Understood, *Superman III.*"

"This is *Battlestar Galactica II* requesting latest Nielsen."

"*Galactica II*, you are on control-tower frequency."

"Oops, wrong channel, sorry."

"*Star Trek II: The Wrath of Khan* from control tower."

"*Star Trek II.*"

"Paramount requests, are you coming in on schedule?"

"Control tower, how can we come in on schedule if necessary to hold for special effects at sixteen million? Suggest rewrite screenplay or revise the producer or both."

"Stand by."

"*Superman III also* standing by, *and* standing by, *and* standing by."

"*Superman III*, this is control tower with figures."

"Go ahead."

"*Superman II* has reached 229,870,000 and holding."

"Holding how?"

"Holding beautifully."

"*Terrific. Superman III* is now—"

"Control tower—"

"Control tower—"

"Control tower—"

"Control tower—"

"*Superman III* is coming in for immediate landing."

"Negative, *Super III*. Theatre Owners of America do not want you in before December 1983."

"Tell TOA to go DTT. *Super III* is *coming in*."

"Control tower, *Snatchers II* is *also* coming in—on two spores."

"Control tower, *Star Trek II: The Wrath of Khan* is coming in—*without* special effects."

"Ditto *The Late Great Planet Earth*."

"Control tower, *Star Wars III* is leaving Sirius and coming in."

"Leaving where?"

"Sirius, the dog star."

"*Which* star?"

"*Dog . . . dog . . .*"

"Control tower, did somebody just call *The Swarm?*"

"Negative. Buzz off. This is the control tower. Attention *Superman III, Star Wars III, Star Trek II, Body Snatchers II, The Late Great Planet Earth*. You cannot *all* come in at the same time. Repeat, *cannot, cannot*."

"Hey, you can all come *here* if you want to. Come on in."

"Who *is* that on the frequency?"

"You can all come here at the *same* time on the *same* heading at the *same* altitude, and there's ice on the runways and a power failure and a cloudburst and a cyclone, and we're all about to have *massive heart attacks*, so come on in."

"Who *is* this, who *is* this?"

"*Airport '84*, a Vincent Couldbe-Gene Moustache production. Hurry!"

The Producer

After a long restful sleep, untroubled by thoughts of industry strikes, rising unemployment, falling box-office receipts, and other cares that were besetting most motion-picture producers, Courtney B. Einfeld awoke in the bedroom of his Sunset Strip apartment, gazed out of the windows at the warm California sunshine and the blue California sky, and thanked his lucky stars, and his superstars, too, that he lived and worked in the land of the lotus. Dressing himself in the casual garb that had been his Hollywood uniform for many years, he looked with pride into the mirror, knowing with the same certainty that he felt about his skills in the picture business that he looked pretty goddamn good for a guy his age. Blue-eyed, distinguishedly gray, and deeply tanned, Einfeld exuded rugged vitality and prosperous self-assurance. About him there was the aura of a man who could handle a twenty-five-million-dollar production as easily as he could stir a cup of coffee, and who could make as much of a production out of a cup of coffee as he could out of a twenty-five-million-dollar picture.

"This is cold, and it's much too weak," he complained to the manager of the Westward Ho supermarket, where he took his morning pick-me-up.

"Sorry about that, Mr. Einfeld," said the manager, whose name was Jerry Seidell. "Let me make you some fresh."

"And where's the melba toast?" Einfeld demanded.

The manager shrugged. "I guess we're all out. It's kinda late, you know."

Einfeld said nothing, but privately he felt scorn for the man. If he made pictures the way this man ran a supermarket, he'd soon be out of the picture business running a supermarket. Sidling over to the magazine and newspaper rack, he took down *Daily Variety* and the *Hollywood Reporter* and read them both from cover to cover, though he ignored the gossip columns. Einfeld was a serious film man, serious about his profession, interested now only in noting those pictures that were going into production, or were *in* production, or were heading for release. Analyzing the subject matter, cast, and director of each film, he concluded that not a single one of them had a prayer, and without allowing himself to feel smug about it, he congratulated himself for not having fallen into the trap of piloting any of these doomed ventures himself.

He returned the trade papers to their rack and left the supermarket, but not before cashing the Paramount check which had arrived in the morning mail. Though it was insignificant in size, it brought a look of awe to Jerry Seidell's face as he initialed it.

"Geeze, did *you* produce *My Heart's in the Valley?*"

Einfeld smiled coolly. "Paramount seems to think so."

"I remember it like it was yesterday. It used to be my favorite picture."

"Still paying off," Einfeld said on his way out. Maybe tomorrow the son of a bitch would have enough respect for him to see that there was melba toast on the plate, and coffee that was worthy of being called a customer service, instead of an insult.

He walked across town at a brisk pace, shunning the slothful ways of the Mercedes, Rolls, and BMW drivers who whizzed by en route to nowhere. While *they* guzzled gas and expended every kind of energy but their own, Einfeld toned his muscles, firmed his body, expanded his chest and lungs, and vitalized his heart, a heart that any producer worth his salt *needed* in order to survive the intricacies and frustrations of the ever-changing industry.

Arriving at the Doubleday bookstore in Beverly Hills, Einfeld stopped outside the entrance, removed from its display rack the latest issue of weekly *Variety*, and carefully studied the performances of the fifty top-grossing films in the nation, with particular attention to the relationship of box-office receipts to the number of theaters showing each picture. Following the fortunes and misfortunes of his competitors was just one of many activities Einfeld engaged in each day in order to maintain whatever edge he could as a picturemaker.

He went inside the bookstore, exchanged greetings with the manager and sales personnel, and immediately began his careful perusal of the hundreds and hundreds of volumes on the display tables and on the bookshelves and in the stacks on the floor. He usually started with fiction, worked his way clockwise to nonfiction, then back to fiction again, reading only the plot information on the dust jackets of the books. It was all his highly trained mind and well-developed sense of smell needed really to determine which book, if any, was a movie possibility. Few books ever were. And fortunately for him (he would observe to himself with an inner smile), those few that *were* possibilities had usually been snapped up in galley form long before, saving *him* from the disaster that inevitably overtook ninety-nine percent of their translations to the screen.

Some producers had lavish office suites at the studios, or in Century City. They employed braces of secretaries, and small armies of readers to cover all existing material and synopsize it for them. But to Einfeld, this was needless extravagance, expensive window dressing. The only money well spent, he felt, was money spent on something you could see on the screen, an uncharacteristically responsible attitude in today's self-indulgent Hollywood, an attitude that Einfeld steadfastly maintained no matter whose money it was, even his own.

He was exhausted when he finally left Doubleday. This was the most wearying aspect of filmmaking, this cautious selection and rejection of material. He hadn't found anything today that had aroused his interest. Without their knowledge, more than six hundred authors in many parts of the world had been said no to by Courtney Einfeld. Exhausted or not, he nevertheless found himself possessed of sufficient energy now to continue across town, pushing his way through hordes of tourists and shoppers mindlessly obsessed with buying things they did not need with money that could have been better spent financing an Einfeld film.

Arriving at Wilshire Boulevard, he entered the showrooms of Hillcrest Cadillac, sought out John Ripple, and said to him, "John, I'm still thinking about that El Dorado. Maybe I better drive one again."

"Gee, Mr. Einfeld," the salesman said, "I don't have an El Dorado demo in the house, only a Coupe De Ville."

"I'll try that then," said the film producer.

"How soon can I have it back?"

"Tomorrow morning?"

"Before noon though. *Please*, Mr. Einfeld?"

He drove out to Universal, took a table in the café, made notes with pad and pencil concerning some of the stuff he had covered at Doubleday, nodded to Lew Wasserman, who apparently failed to see him, smiled at several writers, actors, and producers who passed by on their way out, and finally ordered coffee when the waitress who had brought him rolls and butter started bothering him. Einfeld had a reputation for being wily and closemouthed about his production activities, far too shrewd to divulge anything about work in progress. No one even bothered anymore to ask him what he was doing, confining their greetings to a nod of the head or a discreet "Hello, Courtney."

Shifting his endeavors to the restaurant at Burbank Studios, Einfeld had a nourishing bowl of minestrone soup, after a brief round of table hopping with the secretaries to Alan Ladd, Jr., and Frank Price, careful to extend his very best wishes to their respective bosses (Einfeld was not a man to ignore the amenities), and for dessert, at MGM/UA, he picked idly at the pound cake of Frank Rosenfelt's assistant while discussing the future of laser discs versus videocassettes in the home-entertainment picture. Einfeld's views were always delivered swiftly, compactly, and succinctly. Because he valued his own privacy so highly, he respected the privacy of others, too, and never spent more than five minutes at anyone's table, particularly if the person seemed preoccupied, restless, or otherwise engaged. Sometimes, he left after less than a minute.

He drove now to Westwood Village to see the new Richard Pryor film that was doing so phenomenally well at the box office. Einfeld preferred the public screening room of a movie house to the conventional private screening rooms that other producers used at the studios or in their homes. He could not understand their shortsightedness. It was so obvious to him that one could so much more effectively analyze a film if a paying audience were present.

"Go right in, Mr. Einfeld," the theater manager said to him. "Good to see you again."

Einfeld enjoyed the film, and understood why Richard Pryor had never come to *him* with the project, had probably never even considered him. Richard Pryor, like so many of the others, would have known that this was not a Courtney Einfeld film, and that Einfeld would have turned it down. Nobody liked to be turned down, especially by Courtney Einfeld. Better not even to think of him, out of self-protection if nothing else. Einfeld understood and respected their respect for him. Still, he was glad he had screened the picture. It had actually made him laugh out loud. And few things *ever* made Einfeld, a serious picturemaker, laugh out loud. Not these days anyway.

It was getting dark when he got out of the theater, and he had to take many chances with the Coupe De Ville in heavy traffic in order to get back to his apartment, shave, change clothes, and make it to the Darryl F. Zanuck Theatre at Twentieth Century-Fox in time for the preview. He had already seen the picture, but he wanted the opportunity to tell Bubbles Hennessey in person how much he liked it, because he knew how valuable his enthusiasm would be to the morale of the new young president of the studio, and he particularly enjoyed the beef Stroganoff that was usually served at the buffet supper afterward.

Miss Hennessey wasn't there, it turned out, so he told several minor studio executives and two members of the publicity department what a terrific picture they had, knowing that *their* morale deserved a boost, too. And he did not allow himself to be disappointed by the absence of beef Stroganoff from the menu. He ate the chicken curry uncomplainingly, with grace, and took an extra dessert home with him in a paper napkin. He did not want to miss the late-late show. There was still so much to be done, looking at old movies for new ideas, new movies for other people's errors of judgment, selecting, rejecting, making vital decisions, as he had done all day.

He loved his work. There was nothing he would rather do. From time to time, well-meaning friends would urge him to get into insurance or real estate. "What?" he would say to them. "And give up the picture business?"

At two-thirty in the morning, after putting in an unusually hard day, he turned off the television set and prepared for bed. He felt tired, but satisfied. He hadn't made any rash decisions, hadn't committed himself or anyone else to potential disaster. He believed in biding his time. There was no reason to hurry. No one was exactly *pressuring* him to make a picture. They had too much respect for him for that.

He'd find another *My Heart's in the Valley*. That's what he wanted, had always wanted. And he'd find it all right. Even if it took *another* twenty-two years.

Strike While
the Irony Is Hot

I'm sitting here in the middle of the Great Actors' Strike of the Nineteen Eighties, hoping that by the time anything I say gets into print, the strike will be over. I am sitting at my computer, thinking that perhaps any machine that can beat me so consistently at checkers ought to be able to tell me how the strike will work out, *when* it will work out, and what life will be like in the entertainment industry when it's all over. I'm getting lonesome sitting in front of this computer, but who else do I have to talk to? Practically everyone I know here in Hollywood is on strike. I'm not allowed to talk to *them* and they're not allowed to talk to *me*, because I'm working on a movie. What I mean is, I'm *writing* a movie. Actually, I'm not writing a *movie*, I'm writing a *screenplay*. It may *become* a movie, or it may not. You can't make a movie without *actors*, and who enjoys removing a scab? Not me.

My wife and I would like to see our friends. We'd like to have some of them over to the house for dinner. Better yet, we'd like to go over to *their* houses for dinner. But we can't do either. It just wouldn't work out. I'd have to sit there all night with my mouth shut (except for eating purposes). I got a prior ruling on this from the Screen Actors Guild. They said I'm preparing a movie; therefore I'm not allowed to talk to actors. I said I'm a writer, not a producer. They said I *talk* to my producer; therefore I could be suspected of indirectly *interviewing* my friends for him under the guise of socializing with them. I said, what if I stop *talking* to my producer, would that help? They said no, we can't get involved in that, because that could be interpreted as being in restraint of trade.

So here I am (and my wife, too) isolated, alone, deprived of human contact (except for each other). It's all my fault, too. Years ago she warned me that I was "going Hollywood," that I wanted to associate only with actors, especially stars. I thought it was actresses she was really concerned about but I was wrong. She meant *thespians* in *general*. Someday I'd regret it, she warned me, and she was right.

I sit here in this ghost town, this wasteland, talking to my computer and getting beaten at checkers. You don't know what it's like in the middle of the Great Actors' Strike of the Nineteen Eighties, because *you're* already in the future, reading *this*. It's all *right* where *you* are. To you, it'll be like nothing ever happened. But in your past, it was really like I'm telling it. *You've* got *Annie, Poltergeist,* and *E. T.* to keep you warm. You've got Woody Allen, Neil Simon, Goldie Hawn, Steve Martin, Charlotte Rampling, Elizabeth McGovern, and Dudley Moore. I've got my computer.

It's terrible in the here and now. No new films are being made. An already lean year is going into *anorexia nervosa,* and the industry is getting *nervosier* every day. Movie audiences have nothing fresh to see, so they're getting fresh with the usherettes. The critics have nothing to criticize, so they're criticizing each other. Producers have nothing to produce except *little* producers. Directors are hanging out on street corners, directing traffic. Studio executives are taking meetings, but only with their husbands. Those who don't have one are traveling to other studios to see what their next office is going to look like. Agents can't make deals, so they're throwing gin games to their hungry clients. Cutting rooms are deserted. The editors are all at home cutting out paper dolls. Cinematographers with no sets to light up are switching to cigarettes. Theater owners are playing reruns of the sequels to the pictures they've already rerun. . . .

Where will it all end? I ask my computer.

It's your move is all my computer will say.

You mean *I'm* supposed to be able to see the dawn of that new day, when the actors and writers and directors and producers and all the other creative contributors will have won that precious piece of the gross in pay television and videocassettes?

It's your move, chubby checkers replies.

I start thinking about what it will be like. I begin to picture it. I see the producers producing. I see the writers writing. I see the directors directing. I see the actors acting. But wait a minute. What is that I see on pay television? What is that the cables are cabling? What is that the videos are cassetting? Piece of the gross? Piece of the gross of what? *What* piece of the gross?

I'm looking at every pay television channel. Each one of them is running only the "NFL Game of the Week" (and grossing ten million bucks apiece). And each channel is showing a *different* "NFL Game of the Week," because who's to say which game *isn't* the "Game of the Week"? Ten pay television channels. Ten "Games of the Week." How does SAG get in on the gross? Who are the actors here? The quarterback who fakes a handoff and throws a pass? The punter who falls down untouched and claims Roughing the Kicker? That's acting? Or is it?

Well, is it?

It's your move, says my friend.

What about the Writers Guild of America? How do *they* get *their* slice of the pie that I'm tasting on every channel? Who's the writer? The coach who writes the game plan? The assistant who draws the diagrams on the blackboard at the half? Writers writing with *chalk*?

The Directors Guild has an even *bigger* problem trying to get its hunk. The only directors I see on this scene are the stadium ushers. Stretching it a little bit, you might be able to make a case for the middle linebacker. He does tell the defense how to play it.

There's no doubt about it—winning the Great Strike is one thing, but getting your guild members into the NFL is a Rozelle of a different color, and not so sweet. And getting the NFL to join your guild is even worse.

I sit before my computer, and I brood about this vision I'm having, and I think, For *this* my wife and I had dinner alone for *how* many months is it? Is this all that comes of all those weeks of sacrifice in which directors were reduced to making home movies and the musicians did nothing but fiddle around?

I need better than that, I tell my computer. Give me something to live on until the real future gets here.

–' - — —, the computer replies.

OK. There's still the videocassette market. Let's not forget that. It's a *biggie*, and everyone is *in* on it now, right?

Right.

So what's the number-one-selling videocassette in the new order of things and who gets what from whom? The answer is

Better Blintzes with Julia Wild, and so far, nobody is getting anything from anybody (unless you want to count all the better blintzes that twenty-one million people are now eating, and the $37 million gross in the coffers of the distributor). As for the guilds? *Bubkes.*

The whole matter is in the hands of a National Arbitration Committee, and will be for years. The distributor claims that Julia's on-camera cooking is off the cuff and off the wall. "Just look at her cuffs," they say. "Look at the walls." The Writers Guild refuses to buy that. They claim that there are *recipes* involved, that this constitutes scriptwriting, and that each blintze must be classified either as an original screenplay (material written directly for the videocassette player) or as a screenplay adaptation (based on material previously cooked in another medium). SAG, on the other hand, contends that the whole show is a *put-on,* that it isn't whether the blintzes are light as a feather or thick and rubbery that matters, it's the way Julia talks and laughs and coos as she cooks that counts, and *that's a performance.*

When you consider that number one on the charts is *Better Blintzes,* it comes as no surprise that number *two,* and right behind it, is *Lose Thirty Pounds in a Week with Lenny Levine.* When I tell you that both of these hot-selling cassettes are put out by the same distributor (they've got the American Belly coming and going), it should come as no surprise either that *Lose Thirty Pounds in a Week with Lenny Levine* is another sad story for the winners of the Great Strike.

Script?

"*One* two three four, *one* two three four, *one* two three four, *one* two three four. . . ."

Levine doesn't *use* writers. A magnificent specimen at ninety-three, he can still count all by himself. So that takes care of the WGA.

Directors?

"I don't need one," says Levine. "After eighty-six years of doing this, and my cartilage better than it was when I was seventy-two, nobody is going to tell *me* how to do knee bends."

So much for the DGA.

That leaves SAG. And it sure does. *Out.*

"When *I* say, '*One* two three four, *one* two three four,' *I* mean it, I'm *not acting*, and that's why you lose the thirty pounds, because *you know* I'm not acting. So why should I join the Screen Actors Guild and give away a big piece of the action? I'd rather *starve* first. Hey, don't quote me on that. The public might catch on that there's a quicker and cheaper way to lose weight."

You know what? I've had enough of this. I think I'm going to get up now and go out on a picket line. Maybe I can keep this strike from ever being won. Because if they never agree to give us a piece of the gross, how will they ever be able to screw us out of it?

Soon to Be
a Three-Year-Old
Major Motion Picture

The phone rang. It was my agent.

"What are you doing with yourself these days?" he asked, as though it were any of *his* business.

"Watching the very latest in home entertainment on cable TV," I said. "Meaning any movie that's three years old or older."

"Haven't you got anything better to do with your time?"

"Well," I said, "I did just put the finishing touches on a new novel."

"New *novel*? I didn't know you were writing another one."

"Uh-huh."

"You weren't writing one the *last* time I talked to you."

"That was two weeks ago," I said.

"Must be a slim little thing, huh?"

"It's in longhand now," I said. "It should come to about seven hundred pages in manuscript."

He brightened. "I'll send a messenger over right away. We'll have it typed for you right here in the office."

"That should save me a couple of grand," I said.

"Anytime," he said.

"How about the last time?" I said.

He changed the subject to his favorite. "Think there's a possible movie in it?"

"I wouldn't know," I said. "If there were, I suppose it would be what you people call a woman's picture."

"Now you're talking," he said. "What's it about?"

"Oh, there are these two beautiful women, both in love with the same man . . ."

"Right."

"Then all three get eaten by a huge mechanical shark . . ."

"Uh-huh."

"And when it appears that it's all over for the two girls and the guy, the mechanical shark returns, and we realize then that it isn't really a shark, it's an extraterrestrial spaceship . . ."

"Gotcha."

"It lands on Runway 28 at JFK airport, the mouth opens up, and out walks our guy holding the hands of the two girls . . ."

"Oh, good, I'm glad the women are back in the picture."

"They're not," I said. "He's got only their hands."

"Oh," he said.

"Before our hero can get away from the airport, it gets hit by a hurricane, an earthquake, and a raging fire in the tower started by an angry teenage girl with telekinetic powers. Everyone gets trapped at the airport: two feuding ballerinas; a sometime actress who has just been deserted by still another boyfriend; her sharp-tongued, precocious young daughter who had hoped to be the first twelve-year-old hooker north of New Orleans, but who had been turned down because they hadn't been impressed with her curves and who was now the only twelve-year-old ever to pitch for the Oakland A's with a good inside curve, a good outside curve, and no fastball whatsoever; a shy young spinster and an Italian heavyweight fighter whose only ambition is to go the distance with her; oh, and this neurotic little guy with horn-rimmed glasses who has this tall, dippy girlfriend called Lahdeedah with a craving for chocolates . . ."

"Lahdeedah?"

"What's wrong with Lahdeedah?" I demanded.

"Nothing, nothing. What's in a name anyway?"

"Now, where was I when you interrupted me?"

"There were all these characters trapped at the airport . . ."

"Yes, and it's a Saturday-night and this Italian has a *fever* . . ."

"The fighter?"

"Please don't interrupt. It's the kind of fever that gives him the *shakes*, and he's *very* embarrassed, so to save him from humiliation, Lahdeedah, who, by the way, is really a stewardess for Braniff General, herds everyone into the stewardesses' lounge of Braniff General where the airline's entertainment personnel, known as the BGs, are waiting out the hurricane, the earthquake, and the tower inferno by humming little ditties through their combs. Pretty soon everyone is dancing and turning the place into a disco, and the Italian with the shakes does it so much better than anyone else that he naturally wins first prize, but he realizes that it was an empty win because he never could have done it without the fever, so he gives the prize back and walks out with Lahdeedah, and goes the distance with her. . . ."

"Where?"

"In the economy section of a 747 stranded at the bottom of Jamaica Bay."

"How the hell do they get down *there?*"

"In a gray submarine that accidentally sinks while the two are in the conning tower taking refuge from the hurricane."

"What happened to the shy spinster?"

"Nothing yet. She's jealous as the devil and, later on, she gets into a kicking, slapping, and hair-pulling battle with one of the feuding ballerinas."

"And the *other* ballerina?"

"*He* makes a play for the smart-ass twelve-year-old girl who pitches for the Oakland A's, which really riles the kid's mother because she doesn't want to see her bad-news daughter break training . . ."

"I get it."

"Meanwhile, the mothership, which in the beginning we had thought was a *shark*, takes off from Runway 28 with a diverse group of folks trapped at the airport and goes off into the night sky in search of the eye of the hurricane. They must find this eye and destroy it before it destroys not only the world but the whole damned galaxy. They dub the evil storm Hurricane Barf, after one of the characters taken aboard the mothership, a husbandless woman who vomits into a sidewalk trash can every time a man jogs out of her life . . ."

"That's very good . . . romantic . . . I like that."

"So then there's this big battle up there in the sky. Is the mothership going to get Barf before Barf gets the galaxy? It's quite exciting, and I don't want to spoil it for you. But I *will* tell you that the husbandless woman meets an artist, a painter, aboard the mothership during the war with Barf, and it appears that nothing can stand in the way of their love for each other except that she is unduly amused by his British accent and by the bristly hairs of his beard, and every time he tries to kiss her she starts to giggle and this infuriates him, because what she doesn't know is that he uses his beard to *paint* with, and finally he tells her with his British accent that he is going to walk out on her if she is going to insist on making his beard something to throw up to him every time they kiss, so she giggles and he walks out on her (it's a really *big* mothership), but she decides not to go along with him, she wants to be independent, so she rips out the wall on which he has created an abstract painting with his beard, and she staggers around with the wall in her hands, waiting for someone to help her with it, but they all just look at her as though to say, you're so independent, go carry your own goddamn painting."

"For what it's worth, I agree with them," he said.

I ignored him. "Meanwhile, back at the airport, while Lahdeedah and the Italian are being rescued from the bottom of Jamaica Bay, the neurotic little guy with the horn-rimmed glasses realizes that his dippy girlfriend has disappeared, and, knowing of her insatiable craving for chocolate candy, he wanders through the windblown, quake-shattered, fire-ravaged airport, from one magazine-and-candy counter to another, looking for Miss Hershey. Suddenly he finds himself face to face with the moving lens of a closed-circuit TV camera, which is one of many such security devices throughout the building. Thinking it's a *movie* camera, the neurotic, horn-rimmed guy, crazed and emotionally undone by all the wind and the smoke and the temblors and the comb-humming of the BGs and too much looking for Miss Hershey, peers into the camera and goes into a crazy, far-out, funny monologue about a girl clarinetist who calls herself Buster

Keaton. An airport guard watching the monitor in the security room thinks he is seeing the beginning of the latest
Steve Woodpecker film—"

"Steve Woodpecker?"

"—So he turns on the videotape recorders connected to *all*
the monitor screens, including the one hooked up with the
outside camera that points to the sky, and pretty soon he's got
on videotape all the action, including the Barf war, and the
independent woman with a wall but no marriage certificate
in her hands, and the Italian who went the distance on the
747, and Lahdeedah who is so mixed up she doesn't know
whether she should be looking for a candy bar or for the guy
with the horn-rims, and the feuding ballerinas with the
black-and-blue shins, and the actress who is so tired of saying
so long to men that she acts mean and nasty when this man
with a beard and a British accent walks in claiming he's a
painter fresh off a mothership who just gave a girl the heaves,
and the twelve-year-old who broke training and lost her
curves to love tells her mother to be nice to the man, he has
an apartment, and the shy spinster takes back her Italian, a
little rocky but none the worse for his going the distance, and
horn-rims finds Lahdeedah and they get married and have a
baby and decide to call it Oscar, but it turns out to be a girl
so they name it Julia."

"Julia? Why not Annie?" He always asks such stupid
questions.

"Tell me," I said. "Do you think there's a movie in it?"

"Frankly," he said, "I counted eighteen of them."

So I hung up on him.

Comes the
Video Revolution . . .

"Hello, Worldwide?"

"Looking right at you, sir."

"Troubleshooting, Western Hemisphere?"

"At your service, sir. What seems to be the trouble? You look concerned."

"I'm not sure, miss. It may be in the Satcom III satellite. It may be in my parabolic dish. It could even be in my Select-amax. I don't know. That's why I'm calling. I wonder if you could either send someone over, or hook into my two-way Amex system via Warnercom and troubleshoot me from over there in London."

"What part of the western states are you calling from, sir?"

"Brentwood. That's in Southern California. The old movie district. I mean, all we ever get to see here are old movies, on the cable systems, of course."

"We have no one in that area right *now*, but I do see that we might have a man in Johannesburg who *might* be able to make it onto your screen later in the afternoon."

"That would be fine."

"In the meantime, want to talk to me about some of your problems?"

"Yes. First of all, tell me: Is *Kramer vs. Kramer* a heavyweight title fight, or is it by any chance a Davis Cup match?"

"Neither, sir. It's a movie . . . a domestic comedy drama."

"Ah hah. What about *Star Wars?* That *is* the Oscar telecast, isn't it?"

"No, sir, it isn't."

"I knew it. I *knew* it. I either keep hitting the wrong satellite, or one satellite keeps spilling over into another. I *told* my wife that Dr. Albert Schweitzer was not in *Saturday Night Fever*, but she wouldn't believe me."

"How long have you been experiencing this disturbance, sir?"

"I think the first time I sensed something was wrong was a couple of weeks ago. I was watching the Northern Hemisphere transmission of *Gone With the Wind* via CFN, and noticed that the love scenes between Scarlett O'Hara and Rhett Butler were just a *little* bit steamier, had just a *little* bit more total nudity than I had remembered."

"Perhaps it was your memory, sir."

"That did occur to me. Until the final scene came, and Rhett walked out on Scarlett for the very last time. He didn't say, 'Frankly, my dear, I don't give a damn.'"

"He didn't?"

"No. Instead of 'damn,' he used another word."

"And what was that, sir?"

"I'd rather not *say* it, if you don't mind."

"Why don't you just punch the word out on your Qube?"

"All right. Here goes. . . . Got it?"

"Indeed I do, and I'm *very* sorry about that, sir, and on behalf of Worldwide, I want to apologize to you. Quite obviously your dish was either programmed to a slightly inaccurate azimuth reading, or your receptor angle was a hair too wide, because according to Master Control, which I have just interfaced as we were talking, at precisely the moment that Rhett Butler's line of dialogue was coming to an end via the equatorial Satcom, Hot Box Office, or HBO, as you chaps call it, was delivering *Ecstasy Girls* to the 800 block of Brooktree Avenue in Gaslight, Louisiana, via the Antarctic starcom, which is in a slightly higher orbit but a not appreciably different perigee."

"Well, doesn't that seem to indicate that I'm picking up bits and pieces of HBO when I'm supposed to be locked into the Classic Film Network?"

"Indeed it does, sir. May I ask what kind of dish you are using?"

"Sears Roebuck. Twenty-inch."

"Fine product. Quite selective. Normally, you should be having no adjacent-satellite interference."

"Just between you and me, miss . . ."

"Of course, sir, we're on scramble."

"Is there any way I might be able to pick up *more* of Hot Box Office than just the *fringes?* I mean, without having to move to the southwest United States?"

"Are you saying that what you'd really like is to be able to receive *both* Classic Film Network *and* Hot Box Office, is that correct?"

"Well, *almost,* but not *exactly,* and I do hope you won't misconstrue my motivation. It seems to me that I'd have far less trouble receiving *one* satellite *perfectly* than always struggling to keep two of them separated, and it might as well be HBO, inasmuch as those *happen* to be my brother-in-law's initials. I mean, why not? Only last night I was watching

Citizen Kane on CFN, and you wouldn't *believe* what Kane said on his deathbed instead of 'Rosebud.'"

"Wait a minute, don't tell me."

"You'll never guess."

"I don't have to guess. It's coming up on my CRT right now. . . . *Oh*, my goodness. Oh, my *goodness* . . ."

"Goodness had nothing to do with it, dearie."

"No, that's *tonight*, sir, on the CFN Mae West Festival. What *you* were getting, cross modulated, so to speak, with *Citizen Kane*, was the climax of a live exhibition out of Macao—"

"A live exhibition? . . . Macao? . . ."

"That's right. Via Adult Triple-X-Com microwaved into Run Run Schwartz—Far East."

"Say, I never heard of *that* one before. It sounds . . . educational. I suppose fringe is all I could hope for at that distance."

"One never knows, sir. After all, you have a Neiman-Marcus in your area. Line of sight, too."

"Only a few miles away."

"Well, sir, if you don't mind the thirty-five-thousand-dollar gulp, you *might* be able to find a dish that would do it for you. Would you like me to run a test purchase while you wait?"

"You're being *very* nice."

"Thank you. Stand by, please. . . . Here we go. . . . Here we go. . . . Neiman-Marcus, Beverly Hills, third floor. Model 742B12 . . . Heading, one-sixty north, forty-eight west, twenty-eight above the horizon. . . . There we go. . . . There we go. . . . Perfect. . . . Oh, yes, perfect . . . Hong Kong. This one is out of Hong Kong. . . ."

"Can I see it?"

"Another live one . . . *Very* live one. . . . They call it 'Rocking the Sampan'. . . ."

"Can I see it?"

"Good . . . *gracious* . . ."

"Can I *see* it please?"

"It just ended. . . . *Whew.* . . . It's all over now. . . ."

"Hello? . . . Hello? . . ."

"I'm sorry. You were saying, sir?"

"Am I in range with that dish? That's all I want to know. *Am I in range?*"

"Absolutely, sir."

"And will it pick up Hot Box Office, too?"

"Easily, sir."

"Then I'd like to initiate purchase and installation immediately."

"Very well, sir. Your bank, please?"

"First Interstate. Branch 177."

"SSN?"

"What?"

"Social Security number."

"One-one-three, oh-seven, eight-one-three-seven."

"Stand by please. . . . Good . . . Good . . . Perfect. . . . Credit cleared. Installation Tuesday, three P.M. Space requirement, half an acre unobstructed."

"No problem. Now, about Triple-X-Com, do I need an unscrambler?"

"You need more than that, sir. Run Run Schwartz has an agreement with the ICC that no one under the age of forty will be permitted to receive Triple-X."

"That lets *me* in."

"I'm afraid you'll *still* have to punch your Freedom of Information button, sir."

"Don't you believe me?"

"If you'll punch it, please?"

"There."

"Well . . . you certainly *were* being truthful, and *then* some."

"No cracks please."

"Now what about your wife?"

"I'm not permitted to punch her Freedom of Information button. It's in our marriage contract."

"In that case, she'll have to be excluded."

"She won't mind. I just gave her the Julia Child satellite, the Paul Bocuse satellite, and the Cordon Bleu satellite for her birthday."

"Do you still want me to alert our man in Johannesburg about servicing your present installation?"

"That's very kind of you, miss, but you needn't bother. With Hot Box Office and Run Run Schwartz in the sky, I've decided to cancel everything else."

"*Everything?*"

"Everything. Classic Film Network, the Golden Oldies downlink, the Laurel and Hardy transponder, the Mary Pickford uplink, and Eisenstein-to-Bogdanovich-com."

"But, sir, what about *The Battleship Potemkin, City Lights, The Birth of a Nation, Intolerance, 42nd Street,* Olivier's *Hamlet, A Tale of Two Cities?* . . ."

"Frankly, my dear, I don't give a —"

The Realies

.

Perhaps it is too early to know whether we are witnessing a permanent revolution in mass entertainment, or whether we are in the midst of what will turn out to have been a passing trend. There is little we can do really but wait and see, and hope and pray for the best.

It all started so obscurely as to go almost unnoticed, in a small independent movie house in Pittsburgh, more or less as an experiment. The theater owner, one James MacInerney, had observed that his summer audiences, mostly teenagers and small fry, had become so surfeited with a year of horror films, they were no longer shrieking with joyful terror at the slimy, evil creatures on the screen, whether they were from outer space, supernatural, or earthlings. The monsters were getting laughs instead of screams; human decapitations drew hoots and hollers, and ordinary blood-gushing and eating of extremities got titters and chuckles. The kids had gone to the movies in order to be scared out of their wits, and Hollywood was no longer delivering. *Alien VI, Halloween XII, Alice, Sweet and Sour Alice, Night, Dawn, Afternoon, and Sunset of the Living Dead* and such like had finally inured the youngsters to the artificial frights of special effects. Exploding brains were just so much oatmeal. Flowing blood was nothing but the catsup on their hamburgers.

James MacInerney was worried. The jeering and catcalls of his audiences had an ominous ring. If his audiences didn't get the fix they were looking for, bloodcurdling fright and spine-chilling panic, they would begin to stay away in droves, and that would be the end for him and his little popcorn-peddling theater. And so, at a Saturday matinee late in the month of August (a date that will probably be referred to by film historians of the future as the beginning of the beginning), MacInerney suddenly locked all the exit doors after the show had started, and without warning, set fire to the theater.

Like all breakthroughs in the field of entertainment, all firsts, all innovations, all commencements of new genres and new cycles, MacInerney's idea seemed deceptively simple at the time, and attracted far less national attention than one would have assumed. Most movie executives scoffed at his experiment. *Of course* the screams of terror were real. Sure the fright and the panic and the smell of burning flesh and the cries of the victims and the dense clouds of smoke and the gasps of the asphyxiating were more terrifying than could have been achieved with special effects. But was it art, was it filmmaking at its best, or was it just schlock showmanship?

Irving G. Backoff, who had made millions over the decades with horror films that are now considered to be classics, was blunt with his reaction. "What kind of movie business are we getting into when it don't make no difference if the picture on the screen is *Gone With the Wind* or *Psycho* as long as you pour plenty of gasoline on the seats?"

But Backoff had reckoned without MacInerney's foresight

and imagination. The little theater owner in Pittsburgh did not sit back, content to rest on the local front-page story of the fire, or the printed casualty lists, or the brief, one-day TV coverage of the mass burials. With energy and vision, he personally marshaled the twenty-seven survivors of his experiment into a tight, cooperative, and willing group of public-relations enthusiasts who eagerly recounted the real-life thrills and excitement and agonizing fears they had gone through to any journalist or talk-show host who would listen. The nationwide publicity thus garnered came home like bread cast upon the waters, with honey on it. And all the while, very quietly, MacInerney was buying up old movie houses all over the country.

Cleveland was next, and MacInerney was ready. When the Cleveland *Plain Dealer* refused to accept his ads, he personally handed out leaflets to pedestrians on the sidewalks of the city. "Monday night only! Every seat wired with giant firecrackers! When will they go off? Will you be one of the unlucky twelve with *dynamite* under your seat? Show starts at eight, ends at . . . who knows??"

The Cleveland police had their hands full dealing with the mobs that started lining up as early as five o'clock Monday morning. Over two thousand thrill-seekers were turned away, frustrated in their eagerness to risk their lives for a chance at a new and truly scary experience. On Tuesday, the city council revoked MacInerney's theater license, but by that time there was no theater, only a heap of rubble.

Filmland now took its first official notice of the infant trend. A story actually appeared on page three of the *Hollywood Reporter*, only two paragraphs, but a story nevertheless. Seems a theater in Des Moines, Iowa, was doing such remarkable turnaway business with two very old and much-maligned film musicals that a local team of investigative reporters had decided to look into the phenomenon, and had discovered that the manager was spreading reports by word of mouth that, one hour before each show began, three of his hundreds of candy bars on sale in the lobby would be selected at random and surreptitiously laced with cyanide. The next day, a *Variety* stringer uncovered the name of the secret owner of the movie house, one J. MacInerney.

Hollywood sat up in its collective seat. Something was in the air, and if you didn't breathe it in, you'd better get off the pot. Real Life was the name of the new genre. The trade papers soon shortened that to "The Realies," while the old-style horror films were dubbed "Immies," short for "imitations." The special-effects men, yesterday's heroes, began to find doors closing in their faces. Everywhere they went, heads were turned the wrong way, an effect they themselves had created for *The Exorcist*. Bruce McDouglas, once famous for causing two people in the same room to explode simultaneously and become red-and-gray silhouettes on opposite walls, was forced to accept employment as a third-string catcher for the New York Mets. Whitey Glassman, who in his heyday had reduced the entire visible universe to postage-stamp size, was now himself reduced to prepping an act for Vegas, working out at the Comedy Store on the Strip, where audiences had trouble with his esoteric routines until he finally changed his traveling-matte stories to traveling-salesman stories, and went over big.

Warner Communications was the first of the majors to start the ball rolling (in this case, heads), by announcing a remake of *Murders in the Rue Morgue*, with a new wrinkle in distribution. The movie would play only in houses that had been renamed the Rue Morgue, and all ushers and usherettes would be replaced with "specialists" recruited from the outgoing ranks at Dannemora, Leavenworth, Creedmoor, and Joliet. Audiences at individual theaters would not be told beforehand at what point in the film the screen and the entire

theater would be plunged into Stygian darkness. As the ad
campaign put it: "It's the first picture where *you* may become
the star!" The first sneak preview in Pomona, where three
studio press agents, two elderly couples, and a pair of young
newlyweds were lost, was considered so successful that
Warner common stock soared 3½ points on the Big Board
the next morning, before profit-taking set in.

Paramount became the next distributor to bite the bullet.
Ignoring the loud howls of the Theatre Owners of America,
the Gulf & Western subsidiary bought up every new jet pas-
senger plane declared uncertifiable by the FAA, and every
old plane declared nonairworthy by the same government
agency, and formally announced its Theaters in the Sky, inflight movies for courageous collectors of goose pimples, de-
parting every two hours from two dozen major airports
throughout the United States. Within two months, regardless
of the feature film being shown, T.I.T.S. was outgrossing
every land-based theater chain in the country, with atten-
dance rising by 11 percent after the first two crashes.

For a while, Universal Pictures tried manfully to buck the
trend. A spokesman for the company was quoted in *The Wall
Street Journal* as saying: "We believe in profits as much as
the next guy, but we don't believe in playing Russian roulette
with the American people." Several days later, the spokesman was summoned to the Black Tower to a meeting with
the creative heads of Universal, where he was applauded for
his brilliant idea, given a new contract with much heavier
bread, and allowed to announce the new film project
himself.

The subsequent smashing success of *The Deer Hunter II*
was, of course, almost entirely due to the novel twist of giving each member of the audience a handgun with one bullet
in its spinnable chamber. Theater owners all over the country mopped up. But by the time the flick hit the second and

third runs, Universal had decided to raise the odds to one bullet in every *fifty* guns, the ad-pub philosophy being that you can't sell *future* product to an audience that you've already lost.

Twentieth Century-Fox, which many experts credited with having provided the original impetus to the whole horror-picture scene with such entries as *The Omen, Alien,* and *At Long Last Love,* ironically enough dragged its corporate feet for a while, trying to assess the true staying power of the new hunger for Real Life agony. The company dipped a tentative toe in the water by announcing plans to do a "family" musical called *The Sound of Murder,* but dropped the project after ascertaining that neither Manson nor any other members of his clan would be eligible for parole in time for a reasonable start date.

It was then that Fox took the plunge in earnest, with its famed series of live-action extravaganzas called *The Perils of Pauline,* conceived and produced by the former film critic of *Herpes Bizarre.* Biggest winner in the new Twentieth entertainment package was Mel Brooks, live, in concert at the Hollywood Bowl, in a gut-rending, kidney-straining, bladder-bursting send-up of Werner Erhardt, called *PSST,* in which audiences of up to 19,000 were forcibly restrained from going to the bathroom for an entire weekend.

MGM/UA climbed aboard the bandwagon gracefully, without fanfare and without financial risk. "It's the audience that wants the risks, not MGM/UA," said a company spokesman. Shrewdly using its already highly profitable Grand Hotel in Las Vegas, the onetime film-producing giant embarked upon a brand-new concept to reap beaucoup shekels from the cold-sweat and cardiac-arrest crowd, simply selling tickets at ten dollars a head, first come first served, for a rooftop experience called *Push Comes to Shove,* theme of the nightly happening being how many people could be crowded onto the roof of the Grand Hotel before anyone fell off.

Opening night garnered a jam-packed 9,868 for a gross of almost $100,000, with no reported losses, and those figures were soon to be topped many times during the subsequent run, which is still going strong, records being set at 12,121 (with nine over the side) and 14,560 (with thirty-seven cashing in their chips on the courtyard below). The company wisely replaced the customary candy concession with lobby booths selling low-cost life-insurance policies to the chill-chasers, and reportedly cleaned up, despite payoffs to date to over a thousand beneficiaries.

If a prize were awarded for the highest payoff ratio of cash-invested to profits-garnered, Columbia Pictures would have to be declared the winner in the scare sweepstakes. And to nobody's surprise, it was Steven Spielberg's *Close Encounters* that high-scored for Columbia once again, this time through the simple marketing ploy of using a 900-theater nationwide multiple re-release of the SciFi flick with the added, irresistible danger-lure of a guarantee that at some undisclosed moment in the film, a full-scale replica of the mothership would come crashing down on the audience at *every show*. Cost of prints was minimal, old ones being used for 80 percent of the run, and cost of motherships, using hardware salvaged from scrap heaps, auto-wrecking plants and bankrupt plumbing-supply houses, was reputed to be less than $75 for each of the audience-killing 200-pound devices.

Confidential sources within the company say that the idea for the extremely profitable venture came from an underling in the accounting department who, unable to sleep because of excessive fear of being hit by fragments of the breaking-up U.S. Skylab, turned on his TV set to a very late-late showing of *The Phantom of the Opera*, and combined his insomniacal neurosis with the falling-chandelier climax of *Phantom* to produce the crashing mothership notion that was soon giving audiences all over America the kind of excitement they would never forget, and for some of them, unfortunately, the kind of excitement they would never remember.

An independent filmmaker of high repute who insists on anonymity is quietly preparing a film which *he* believes may put an end to the entire trend, a motion picture designed to be truly unconfrontable, a documentary that will be the ultimate in terror. "It will be," he says, "the most horrifying experience any audience anywhere in the world can be made to face."

He has sworn me to secrecy, but I can tell you the title. It will be called *Reality*.

California Cinema School Curriculum, 1983

Degrees Offered in Film: B.A., M.A., M.F.A., MCA

Seminar on Survival in Hollywood (Cinema 48)—12 hours weekly, 4 units. Class limited to 30 students working in close personal confrontations with well-known professionals of the film community, often one-on-one. How-to-Survive Subjects include:

(1) Alibiing one's failures—the art of being creative.

(2) How to shrug off New York *Times* and national news-weekly film reviews through use of hypnosis, TM, Angel Dust, Rolfing, primal scream, Beefeater's, Club Mediter-ranée, life termination.

(3) Proper social deportment to enhance one's reputation after a Major Failure.

(4) How to avoid getting hit by a car following a Major Success.

(5) Learning the Rules. (It isn't enough to have talent, you must also be a former agent.)

(6) How to believe in yourself when everyone else in the film industry thinks you're great.

(7) What to do about Rex Reed without going to jail for it.

(8) How to manipulate your publicity campaign so that you can take credit for pictures that were made by others (the V.P.-in-Charge-of-Production Syndrome).

(9) How to bury your colleagues without an undertaker's license.

(10) Proper dress at dinner parties, and at the studio, when things are going badly for you . . . and when things are going well (an in-depth review of Yves St. Laurent–Salvation Army debates).

(11) On the need to cast off clichéd, stereotypic attitudes by adopting *fresh* viewpoints. Sample lectures: An Appreciation of the Compassion of John Simon . . . The Case for the Tall Agent . . . It Isn't Enough to Have a Good Backhand, Once in a While You've Got to Get a Picture on the Screen.

(12) Career mistakes you must avoid in the selection of the car you drive, the neighborhood you live in, the charity affairs you attend, the doctors you use, the politics you espouse, the men and women you marry, the restaurants you frequent, and, sometimes, the films you make.

(13) Where to get the best and cheapest hamburger in town, in case you flunk any of the above.

Cinematography 1 & 2—for beginners (8mm) and advanced students (Super 8). 4 hours weekly, 2 units. Limited faculty, subject to the availability of recently fired professionals. Areas of instruction include: how to make a virgin director look good; the use of out-of-focus techniques to create audible audience response; underlighting as a method of keeping your work out of the drive-ins; new ways to speed-read the *Racing Form* during the rehearsals; on developing relationships with female stars (whither hand-held); it is not enough to be Scandinavian, you must also have film in the camera.

Editing the Motion Picture *(Cinema 17)*—long hours, unit and a half for overtime. Study range is broad: getting the intentions of the filmmaker on film; getting your *own* intentions on film (the hell with the director); cutting techniques in the editing room; how to be equally cutting on the sound stage; the Moviola as stepping-stone to becoming a director; the director as stepping-stone to becoming a director; it is not enough to be a woman film editor, you must also look good in a white glove; U.S. Army resuscitation techniques for use on new directors after showing them their first rough cut; how to have fun on the cutting-room floor (see *Biology 12*).

The Genre Film *(Cinema 33)*—for students of all genres. Come as you are, no credit, no fund raising. Every type of motion picture receives brief, concise examination. Examples:
(1) The Suspense Film (will it ever get made?)
(2) The Horror Film (it got made).
(3) Science Fiction (the reported grosses).

Film Writing Workshop (see *Psychology A & B*)—56 hours, shared credit. Seven-day seminar designed to blast away the typical screenwriter's fears and phobias stemming from inadequate data and paranoid thinking. Emphasis on: Will they rewrite me? Are they already rewriting me? Will the actors rewrite the director's rewrites? Can I trust the producer? Who shall I turn to? Guest speakers: Dr. Krafft and Dr. Ebing.

Auteur Cinema—for aspiring directors only. 12 hours a week, all the credit. Heavy emphasis on postproduction activities: the press interview; the "Today" show; "Good Morning America"; Griffin, Donahue, and Johnny Carson (the art of making the screenwriter, producer, cast, cinematographer, art director, costume designer, film editor, composer, and 140 technicians disappear). Guest lecturers: Harry Houdini, Jr.; Mandrake the Magician. Sidebar: the auteurist as biblical figure—"An I for an I, a tooth for a truth." (Related course: *Cinema 19*, The Art of the Screenplay—How to Write Directors' Touches.)

So You Want to Be a Producer—A Symposium *(Cinema 00)*—applicants must survive a one-week Outward Bound program in the Himalayas before being accepted. 17 hours daily, 4 units after 3.2 times negative. Subjects explored: Chase National; Irving Trust; Allen & Co.; City National; Manufacturers' Trust; House of Rothschild; House of Cards; B of A; IOU. Guest lecturer: Nick the Greek (I Thought *Horse Players* Were Crazy). Round Table Discussion by Panel of Studio Heads. Theme: It is not enough for a picture to go through the ceiling, it must also go under the carpet. Guest speaker (by remote): Robert Vesco.

Fundamentals of Film Criticism *(Cinema 69)*—to qualify, students must have had at least two years in an institution. 3 hours weekly, 1 unit. Primarily a crash course in Movie Reviewing Made Easy. Emphasis is on six *sine qua non* maxims:

(1) If the writing is bad, the writer did it.
(2) If the acting is bad, the writer did it.

(3) If the direction is bad, the projectionist did it.
(4) If the picture is good, the director did it.
(5) If the picture is a hit, the audience did it.
(6) If the picture is a mystery, the butler did it.

Advanced Acting Techniques for Motion Pictures—a workshop open only to those with previous film-acting experience. Classes conducted by professional film directors when available, subject to the frequency with which they walk off pictures. Only essentials are stressed:

(1) Showing up on the set.
(2) Opening the script.
(3) Saying the lines.
(4) Getting out of the way of the other actors.
(5) Taking the money.
(6) Running.

The Theater Projection Booth Operator as Film Artist—a lecture series open to serious film buffs only:

(1) Where was Moses when the lights went out?
(2) The developing dynamics of sloppy changeovers.
(3) Out-of-sync as an audience arouser.
(4) New classics from old, by switching reels. (Wind With the Gone . . . Who's Virginia Woolf Afraid Of? . . . The Cistorex . . . Swaj . . . Igig.)

Movie-House Management—an executive administration course for students who plan to combine their deep love of films with their business careers. Cinematic appreciation in a breadwinning setting is taught through lectures, textbook studies, field trips, and laboratory experiments in a variety of moviegoing-related experiences:

(1) *Citizen Kane* as affected by a Hershey's-with-almonds environment.

(2) Lowering the incidence of cardiac accidents during the films of Hitchcock and De Palma through the use of poly-unsaturated margarine instead of hot butter on unsalted popcorn.

(3) Sound-deadened candy wrappers for the films of Zinnemann and Buñuel—economic luxury, artistic necessity.

(4) On the need for replenishing inventory before exhibiting the works of Woody Allen and Mel Brooks, with special reference to Pepsi-Cola and Seven-Up. ("An audience that sprays together stays together.")

Cinema Journalism—a brief course tailored for unpleasant, dyspeptic writers of essays on film. Theme: If you can't find anything nice to say, say it.

Tape No. 192

"Look, men, this is no time to panic. Let's have no *geshrying* in the Octagonal office. We should be *used* to attacks like this by now. We've been a whipping boy for the press ever since we stepped out of the nickelodeons and learned to talk. Today we're a front-page story because they have nothing better to print. Tomorrow we'll be as gone and forgotten as yesterday's newspaper. . . ."

"Beg to contradict, sir."

"Stop begging, Cratchett. Just say it."

"This is more than just a story on the front page, chief. We are talking here about a series of investigations by the federal government. We are talking about charges that we have been concealing profits in order to deny filmmakers their rightful rewards and to deceive the American people into believing that they would lose their collective shirts if any of them dared to enter the movie business and become our competitors. These are serious charges, sir, and could bring this building tumbling down in ruins. . . ."

"I thought I told you never to mention *The Towering Earthquake* in my presence again, Cratchett. Especially you, who talked me into making it by promising me that it would be the ultimate disaster. . . ."

"You never listen, chief. I said it would be the ultimate disaster *film*."

"(Expletive deleted)."

"What's wrong, sir?"

"I just scratched my nose again on these goddamned roses."

"What I don't understand is why you stick your face in that flower vase every time you say something, and why you hold the vase up to *our* faces every time we speak."

"It's simple. Not enough people talk to flowers. They smell 'em, but they don't talk to them. I think it's a shame. Flowers have feelings, too."

"I wish the world could know this side of you, sir, instead of knowing only the vulgarity and brutishness."

"If you were on the ball, they *would* know. You'd tell Ron and he'd tell the press. Why don't you send word to him that it's red roses today, only don't say anything about how I scratched my nose on the thorns."

"Got it, chief."

"Now, where do we actually stand on these upcoming investigations? Who is dealing with the auditors? Has anyone tried to get to Solomon and Finger yet?"

"Yes, Chuck had a talk with them yesterday. He warned them that if they audited our pictures any further, they would be endangering national security."

"What did they say?"

"Nothing. Finger gave that Solomon-like smile, and Solomon gave the Finger. Chuck came out bleeding badly."

"Bleeding? From what?"

"The thorns on the roses in the vase they kept holding under his nose."

"(Expletive deleted). We'll hang Chuck out to dry and let him twist in the Santa Ana. My mogulship must never be tainted with the whiff of corruption. Remember, the buck stops here . . . and disappears."

"I'm sorry, sir. I'm afraid the handwriting is on the wall, and the words are obscene. The CIA refuses to interfere with Price Waterhouse."

"Ungrateful bastards. After all the medium-budget films we've done about them, trying to make them look like heroes. The hell with them. We don't need them. Nobody is going to find anything. The money is too well hidden. We'll stand by our annual earnings reports and both sets of books and let them investigate us until their eyeballs fall out. Unless they can find the money, they've got nothing. Zilch."

"Suppose they decide to take up all the carpeting around here, sir?"

"More zilch. I switched the dough. It's now under the *pad*. Think I'm a fool?"

"What if they use acetylene torches on our vaults and private safes?"

"Empty. See this wall behind my desk?"

"You mean the one where you sealed your brother up when you took the studio away from him ten years ago?"

"I've got news for you. He's buried on the backlot now. This wall now contains the profits from our last forty-nine feature films, *without* the sales to television. *That* I've hidden in a ten-thousand-gallon tank under the studio filling station I hope you don't use super unleaded in the Rolls, Cratchett, because there *is* none around here anymore."

"That's all right. I'm into regular unleaded these days. (Sneeze)."

"Gesundheit."

"It's the roses, chief. If you wouldn't hold them so close . . ."

"Now, does anyone else have anything to say about the investigations before we go on to other business? Counselor, you look edgy. What's on *your* mind?"

"I'll wait until the others have had their say, sir."

"Ulrich, how about you?"

"I have a few thoughts, chief . . . all of them bad."

"Well, come over here to the desk and say it with flowers."

"Chief, you remember that huge computer I installed that figured out we owed the writers, directors, producers, and actors three billion seven hundred million in concealed profit participations—?"

"Goddammit, didn't I tell you to give that computer away?"

"I did, I did. I sold it to Kubrick for a dollar. He renamed it Hal and used it in *2001*. . . ."

"So?"

"I completely forgot to erase its memory bank first, and it's back in circulation now. If Hal ever goes before one of those committees and starts talking . . ."

"(Expletive deleted)."

"The other unpleasant tidings, sir, is that we released *Paraldehyde, I Love You* nationwide in seven thousand theaters, and it's killing them dead. The first projection is two hundred million domestic, but it could go to three."

"Let me hear the concealment plan . . . *fast*."

"There *is* none, chief. There's too much to hide. The damned thing is grossing two million a *day*."

"Well, don't just stand there sniveling. Have the money laundered in Acapulco and sent back to us as surplus from our tequila-bottling plant."

"No way. The bottling plant is already making bigger profits than the picture."

"Has anybody found out about this?"

"Not yet, but they *suspect*. I had Ron tell *The Wall Street Journal* that last week's Mexican revenues were a fluke . . . that we made a mistake and put marijuana in the bottles instead of tequila."

"Say, that's not such a bad—"

"No, chief."

"I mean, we could—"

"Chief, *no*. We let you talk us into building the hotel in Miami and then the other one in New Orleans, and *now* look what we face—a raging torrent of cash flow. When word gets out that our third quarter was five thousand percent better than the last ten years combined, the guilds will call emergency meetings, the conglomerates will trip all over each other to take us over, and what's left of this company will wind up being run by the complaint department at Bloomingdale's or the chef at Chock Full O'Nuts."

"What's the participation breakdown on *Paraldehyde?*"

"What's the difference?"

"Answer me, Ulrich."

"Rutt has twenty percent of the net, Goldbaum has five, Traymore has twelve and a half, and Redwood and Newstein each have ten percent of the gross after double negative."

"Beautiful dealmaking. We're saved. Just start paying them what we owe them . . . immediately. *That*'ll relieve the pressure."

"Uh-unh, chief. No can do. Not under the terms of the Palm Springs Covenant."

"(Expletive deleted) the Palms Springs Covenant."

"That's easy to say, but we're signatories, sir. No participation payments allowed unless we're sued and court-ordered, with an obligation to appeal adverse decisions all the way to the Supreme Court."

"So what can the other signatories do to us if we decide to take a walk?"

"Destroy us, that's all, by taking away our only hedge against the unexpected blockbuster. They can exercise their power, by a two-thirds majority, to cancel our right to make *Sorcerer II, Exorcist III, Lucky Lady Meets Mame, The Continuation of At Long Last Love, Heaven's RearGate, Nickels from Heaven,* and *Another One from the Heart.*"

"Don't even *say* it. All right, if that's the way things are, why don't we cancel all twelve pictures on our present production slate?"

"No, chief, no. We need them desperately. They look like big losers."

"Are the budgets big enough?"

"Huge."

"Subject matter?"

"Horrible to hopeless."

"Good. Brief me, brief me."

"Fourteen mil on a space flick with no stars in it, just a lot of special effects and gun battles without bullets."

"No stars, no bullets? Perfect."

"We double-print them in later."

"Terrific. You'll have to double-print the audience in, too. What else?"

"Twenty mil on something about aliens from another world visiting the earth in spaceships."

"Yech. What's it called?"

"I can't even remember the title, it's so long and forgettable."

"Gimme more."

"Let's see, there's a big stiff about truck drivers with CB

radios being chased by a loony sheriff. Bound to go way over, then straight under. And another one about disco dancing, plenty music, plenty costly, *less* than nobody in it. Also, we did a negative pickup, nineteen million dollars' worth no less, on something about a shark. . . ."

"You mean a gambler?"

"No, a *fish*. Can you believe it?"

"(Laughter). Be sure we make up too many prints, a couple of thousand too many. And book it into too many theaters, every dump you can find. I mean, when you got something really bad you gotta put good money after it."

"Marvelous. We may even be able to show a *legitimate* loss, the first one since '33. Men, I think we've got this situation contained. I think we've been overreacting to a second-rate story in a third-rate trade paper. Investigations? They won't be able to touch us."

"Sir?"

"Yes, what is it, counselor?"

"May I say a few words now?"

"If you insist, counselor. But I have to tell you, whenever you say anything, I hear it with my ulcer. How much time is this going to take?"

"I'll need eighteen and a half minutes, sir."

"Proceed, counselor."

"Let me begin by saying there is a melanoma on the mogulship. . . ."

"I'll send it to the dry cleaner's."

"When the judge sentenced Doberman, he told him that he would be willing to reduce the sentence if Doberman would talk. I think he's going to talk, sir."

"He won't talk."

"He might, sir. No man is going to take ninety-nine years lying down, merely for exercising his penmanship on the backs of three checks for a paltry two hundred and twelve million dollars."

"But that money is in our treasury, safe and sound."

"Exactly. Unknown to our stockholders, unknown to anyone . . . the damaging proof that this company is overwhelmingly into enormous profits. You'd have to resign, sir."

"For being part of the cover-up?"

"Bad as that is, I think you could tough it out. But what you'd *never* overcome would be the deep feeling of betrayal on the part of the other signatories to the Palm Springs Covenant. You'd totally lose your base of support. They'd never forgive you for inadvertently revealing that moviemaking is a can't-lose proposition. Not after the billions they've spent convincing the world otherwise."

"Didn't it ever occur to them, counselor, to any of us, that maybe there was no *need* to go to such extraordinary lengths to keep the shipping clerks out of the game?"

"That's easy to say now, sir, with hindsight. But if you will recall, when it all started, we were afraid every garment manufacturer would pull an Evans-Picone, every Motown would turn into a Metro. We were determined to keep the gasoline salesmen and the cigar-store chains and the small-screen merchants and the doctor-and-dentist tax-loss syndicates from taking over the industry. And let's not forget our horribly justified fears that *talent* would be wanting to stick its fingers in the pie, too. No, we *had* to make ourselves appear to be not just sick but *dying*."

"But it was *true* once. We *were*."

"A long time ago. But we were terminally healthy and didn't know it. Once we started getting well, there was nothing we could do to stop it. We got weller and weller. We *had* to take desperate measures, sir. It was no longer enough to hope that Canby and Kael and Crist and Simon and Reed and Shalit and Sarris and Farber and the Eastern literary establishment could do it *for* us. The more scorn they heaped on us, the more people went to the movies. . . ."

"Why didn't we just make lousier pictures?"

"We *did*. They broke all the old records."

"Then why didn't we make *good* ones?"

"We did that, too. And *they* broke the new records of the lousy ones."

"Are the eighteen and a half minutes up yet?"

"Not yet, sir."

"Oh God. . . ."

"Speaking of that one, sir . . ."

"*I don't want to hear another word about it.* Everyone in this room *swore* to me that it was *safe*, that no one would go to see it. It burns my ass. . . ."

"Swearing won't help, sir."

"Then what *will*? You've got three more minutes."

"Take care of Doberman."

"What?"

"It's the only way."

"It would be wrong, but all right. How much?"

"Not money. That's not what it would take."

"Then what?"

"Offer him the mogulship."

"Mine?"

"Yes."

"But what about me? What would become of *me*?"

"You could retire to San Jose and write your memoirs. Speedy could handle it for you. You'd make a fortune."

"How can I reveal the truth? It would ruin me, ruin all of us."

"Who said anything about the truth?"

"No, I don't like it. My common sense tells me it's too dangerous. And my ulcer tells me your eighteen and a half minutes are up. Thank you, counselor, for nothing. This conversation never took place."

"Oh yes it did, sir. And you can take your finger off that button now."

"What button?"

"That erase button on your desk you've been pressing ever since I started talking. It won't do you any good."

"That's what *you* think, counselor. It'll be your word against mine."

"I'm afraid not, sir. You see, I plan to recount this entire meeting verbatim."

"Yeah? Where?"

"In a highly circulated pamphlet called *Screening Sickness*."

"(Laughter). There won't *be* any highly circulated pamphlet, counselor. Apparently you are unaware that the publisher is at the top of our enemies list."

"Apparently *you* are unaware of the next film on your production slate."

"What's that?"

"Clint Eastwood in *The Smoking Gun*. Ciao, sir."

The Razor's Edge

I sincerely hope that by the time you read this, the controversy over *Dressed to Kill* will have finally died down and the darned movie will have, at long last, disappeared from pay TV. I mean, how long can irate housewives and irate pressure groups and assorted crackpots of the Right and the Left go on yammering in public and writing letters to the editors and sounding off on talk shows about how furious they were with the critics for liking Brian De Palma's film so much when it played the movie houses, and how angry they are at home movie watchers as they continue to lap up the picture on their small screens even at this late date?

One group violently deplores the violence. Another group of bleeding hearts deplores the blood. This group puts a bookmark in its Gay Talese and cries out against the overt sexuality. That group snuffs out the roach and claims the picture is antipsychiatry. Transsexuals claim they are misrepresented. Transvestites demand equal spelling. The

United Auto Workers insist they make backseats for *sitting.* Procter & Gamble gets in a lather over the misuse of *soap.* Schick and Remington charge discrimination against electric razors. Gillette protests the failure to stress the *safety* razor. . . .

Ridiculous. All of it.

Except for the husband's brief stint before the bathroom mirror in the opening scene, *Dressed to Kill* has nothing whatsoever to do with shaving. There is not one foot of film in which Angie Dickinson shaves or gets shaved. In fact, there is visible evidence in the film that she *doesn't* shave. And completely overlooked by everyone apparently is the fact that the writer-director of the film has an oustanding beard himself. If anybody at all connected with this picture could be considered a candidate for getting a shave, it would have to be Mr. De Palma.

One angry cable-watcher writing in to one of the national magazines, or maybe it was to the Boston *Phoenix,* denounced the picture as a ripoff of *Psycho,* completely ignoring the fact that *Psycho* is a black-and-white film while *Dressed to Kill* is in red. Are filmmakers from here on in going to be forced to eliminate all shower scenes from their pictures to avoid charges of ripping off *Psycho?* Are we moviewatchers faced with nothing to look forward to but a succession of dirty pictures with dirty actresses in them? I hope not.

As for psychiatry and psychiatrists, they need no defense from *me.* They can listen for themselves. But the charge that *Dressed to Kill* will cause needy neurotics to live with their problems rather than die with their treatment is like saying that *Gone With the Wind* caused the people of Atlanta to catch cold and give up smoking because they were afraid to light a match. Movies simply do not have that direct, one-to-one impact on their audiences, much as filmmakers would like to believe otherwise.

Any neurotic who sees *Dressed to Kill*—particularly a woman—will probably be sane enough to know that there are all *kinds* of ways of ensuring one's safety during treatment by a male analyst. The easiest method is simply not to *tell* him anything (though that's sort of beating him at his own game, and is ultimately expensive and self-defeating). More practical would be to move his office furniture around so that you can always keep an eye on him, or make *him* lie on the couch while *you* sit up. If he's a straight, decent, safe kind of guy, he surely isn't going to object to being *comfortable*, is he?

Yes, you say, but suppose he is fiendishly clever at concealing his secret proclivities, capable even of fooling his own psychiatrist? Well, it's up to *you*, the potential analysand, to unearth these facts beforehand. You don't just look up a man's medical background, his training. You ask him what his favorite perfume is; you steal a peek into his wardrobe closet; you see if his labels read Brooks Brothers, Carroll and Company, Mr. Guy, or Henri Bendel, Bergdorf Goodman, Rive Gauche. What I mean is, if you have real emotional problems and need help, make sure it is *you* who flips your lid, *you* who wigs out, not him.

Another thing I've learned from this controversy: I'd much rather be listening to Cole Porter's "Miss Otis Regrets" than hearing "Otis Elevator Regrets" over and over again. You'd think, from the hue and cry, that Mr. De Palma had single-handedly set out to destroy the entire elevator-manufacturing industry with *one movie*. What nonsense.

Maybe five or six hundred thousand people will never set foot in an elevator again. But what does *that* mean when you consider the hundreds of *millions* of people who use elevators every single day and will continue to do so, *Dressed to Kill* or no *Dressed to Kill?* Actually, the five or six hundred thousand will *benefit* from the change in life-style. Climbing stairs instead of riding in elevators will strengthen their cardiovascular systems. Here and there, a few will drop like flies, but they would have gone eventually anyway. You can't blame Brian De Palma for *everything.*

Some people *try* to, though. You'd be amazed at some of the attitudes and theories and pronouncements I hear being bruited about on local radio conversation stations and at the more boring cocktail and dinner parties in this film community of ours. And you can be sure that these very same Parlor Paulines flip from one cable channel to another to see the picture again and again.

Dressed to Kill gives blood, our most vital body fluid, a bad name. *Dressed to Kill* gives nurses' white shoes a bad name. *Dressed to Kill* gives subways, sunglasses, sex, marriage, infidelity, police detectives, New York City, telephone answering machines, prostitution, black leather coats, and murder a bad name. *Dressed to Kill* is going to alienate women from modern art because every time they go to a museum now and look at the work of a contemporary artist, they are going to experience this subconscious fear of dropping a glove and picking up a venereal disease.

If these seem like crazy notions to you, you haven't seen *Dressed to Kill* yet, or you haven't read some of the wild letters I've seen in the papers, or heard the mouthings of some of my friends. *Dressed to Kill,* they say, is already taking its toll on the economy. Insurance companies are the hardest hit. Straying housewives are taking off their diamond rings in strange places and forgetting to put them back on with their panties. There has been a four-hundred-percent rise in traffic accidents in the big cities due to cabdrivers not watching where they're going because they're watching where they're coming, in the rearview mirror. Inflation had been leveling off; now it's worsening, because millions of low-income women are taking cabs they cannot afford, instead of buses, trolleys, and metros, in the misguided belief that the women's movement is most effective when it takes a backseat to a man.

Also dangerously inflationary, claim the worrywarts, is the call girl played by Mr. De Palma's wife, Nancy Allen. No $100 hooker *she*. She asks for and *gets* $500 for her services (the hooking, not the acting), and plays her role with such lovableness and sweetness and charm, especially in that black garter belt or whatever it was she was wearing, I wasn't looking, that guys all over the country who might have thought twice before popping for $100 are not going to think even twice before going for the five bills.

Down on the Metal Exchange, specialists say that it was Miss Allen's hooker with a heart of gold, rather than the military conflict in the Middle East, that sent the precious yellow metal soaring before it went into a spin recently. On the face of it, this makes absolutely no sense, because at the very same time Quaker Oats common stock was rising only 1¼ even though an equal number of film fans thought Miss Allen's hooker had a heart of mush.

Of course, no De Palma picture would ever be a De Palma picture if it didn't sent the film buffs scurrying to find hidden homages to Hitchcock in every sprocket hole. *Dressed to Kill* is, to them, a treasure trove, a field day.

The razor? *Spellbound.*

The rain? *Foreign Correspondent.*

The blond-wigged lady in the dark glasses and the long black coat? Karen Black in *Family Plot.*

The elevator? A shower stall without water out of *Psycho.*

Teenager Keith Gordon snooping through the viewfinder of his camera? Jimmy Stewart in *Rear Window.*

Two menacing black men on the subway platform with

Nancy Allen becoming five or six menacing black men when the camera isn't watching? Blackbirds multiplying behind Tippi Hedren in *The Birds*.

The straight-down overhead shot of Nancy Allen in the shower stall? Henry Fonda in his cell in *The Wrong Man*.

Michael Caine on the winding staircase in the psychiatric clinic? Jack the Ripper's hand descending on the balustrade in *The Lodger*.

Nancy Allen accidentally winding up with the bloody razor in her hand, causing the black lady to run away shrieking? Cary Grant in *North by Northwest* finding himself with the murder knife in his hand in the United Nations while onlookers shriek, "Look out. . . . He's got a knife. . . . He did it. . . ." (or whatever the idiot writer had them shriek).

So much for speculation. There is one thing about *Dressed to Kill* on which everyone seems to be in total agreement— the reason why Brian De Palma wears that beard.

Obviously, if he shaved, he'd cut himself to pieces.

Screening Sickness

I don't think any of us, we who toil in the Land of the Lotus, in Tinsel Town, in the Celluloid Jungle (what garbage . . . Come on . . . *We who make movies*), I don't think any of us has given sufficient attention to the hidden toll exacted on our well-being by the singular manner in which we gather to view the creative efforts of our close friends, acquaintances, colleagues, competitors, and worst enemies. One hears much talk of high blood pressure being "the silent killer." But the AMA doesn't seem to give a *damn* about *screening sickness*. Beverly Hills physicians regularly warn their patients to stay out of the sun, it'll give you skin cancer. But never do they warn film folk to stay out of the screening room, it'll give you something worse.

Let me say right now, before you jump to any conclusions or pole-vault to misunderstanding, that I am intending to be serious here. We who are in the film business get to know each other pretty well over the years, some of us intimately, some of us casually, all of us, at the very least, nodding acquaintances. The Los Angeles-Beverly Hills-Bel Air-New York axis is merely a wider angle shot of the location called Hollywood, and no matter where we happen to live and work, we're still members of a company town. And the special occasion on which we see each other most frequently is at screenings.

There are Academy screenings, Writers Guild screenings, Directors Guild screenings, sneak previews, press previews, and studio screenings given by the producer and/or the director and/or the publicity department. These screenings are quite pleasant, quite informal, the price is always right, and the seats are always comfortable. However, these seemingly benign gatherings can give rise to hidden stresses and can bring into play deep-seated inner tensions, the likes of which have been gnawing away at the vital organs of people who work on film the way radium used to eat away the bone marrow and the lives of workers in clock factories.

I think it is unnecessary for me to point out the stresses your heart, lungs, nervous system, and bladder undergo at a screening if the film being shown is one *you* worked on. But I would like to indicate that the imagined hostility of your friends and peers, the conviction that everyone in the room is rooting for the picture to fail, is in *your* head, not theirs. The only chance they have to relax and be happy at that screening is if your picture is good. But if it's bad, they are filled with terrible anxiety throughout the showing, knowing when it's over that they will have to be convincing liars, since you are dumb enough to wait in the rear of the auditorium for their congratulations after the house lights go up.

The very atmosphere in the theater reeks of the dank sweat of uncertain hypocrisy. You smell it, they smell it, and everyone comes off the evening eventually a little less well in body and mind as a result of it. Multiply such evenings by the number we have gone through over the years, and you wonder how any of us are still alive to go through it again.

Such stress would be destructive enough even if that's all there were, even if there weren't, in addition, the lingering, sometimes lifelong effects visited upon humans who feel forced to swallow the truth and tell lies to their friends, time after time after time. The hidden damage to relationships in Hollywood is not caused by the critical remarks people make to each other about each other's films. It is caused by the nice things they say, when they feel the opposite, in the supposed interest of preserving the relationship. It does preserve it, only there's a little less relationship left after the preservation. Not only do we feel diminished by the knowledge that we have suppressed our urge to express the truth, we also resent, be it ever so slightly, the person whose lousy picture we have forced ourselves to praise with the accompanying loss of one square inch of our souls.

I know film people who stay away from screenings, who stand in line at public theaters, rather than face the filmmakers at the fade-out. They feel much safer that way. They figure that, if they don't like the picture, they can always make believe they never even saw it. Of course they run the risk of earning resentment. The other risk you run when you go to a public showing is that you may be seen and recognized without your knowing it. I don't have to tell you the feelings you provoke when you lie about not having seen a friend's picture, and get found out.

We've been talking about pictures that turn out to be horrors. Let's talk about the good ones, the ones that you know are going to "make it" within five minutes after the house lights go down. You can sit there and view such a picture and enjoy it with unadulterated pleasure, totally free of anxiety. You can't wait for it to end so that you can rush to find everyone who was involved in the making of the film to shake their hands and congratulate them and pour out your praise with excitement and honesty in your heart. It feels so good. You tingle all over. The theater reeks with the delightful fragrance of success and happiness. Usually, the strange and unfathomable depression that sets in doesn't come until late the next morning, perhaps just before lunch, and it won't do you any good to think about it. The picture was terrific, and you know it, and all the thinking in the world isn't going to be able to change that.

What is that you're saying? Why not be honest all the time and just say what you think and feel and let the others learn how to handle your truths? That's fine, if you've learned how to handle *their* truths yourself. It's also fine if you happen to be a person who is able to adapt easily to waiting on tables or driving a taxi.

The most stressful screenings in movieland, strangely enough, are the ones most eagerly sought after. You haven't "arrived" in Hollywood, you're not "in," if you aren't invited fairly regularly to the very social, very private screenings in the living rooms of those elitists known collectively as "the Bel Air circuit." That doesn't necessarily mean a highly placed individual living in Bel Air. It can mean anyone from an out-of-work studio head to an out-of-his-head actor.

If you have your own projection room, be it in North Hollywood, Tarzana, or Culver City, you're still the Bel Air circuit because you can get the latest films for nothing and you can make a private deal with the projectionist you have hired for the evening. Your guests can talk back to the screen and jeer at the dialogue and take a vote after reel two to determine whether a majority of you would rather turn off this $24 million production and try one of the other two features you have borrowed for the night as standbys in case the natives get restless.

Let us assume that you, a guest, have had no connection

with the film being shown. That is usually the case, because it would spoil the evening, be far too inhibiting to everyone present, if someone connected with the picture were there.

The first hidden stress that you, a picture person, are exposed to is the subconscious (sometimes conscious) realization, My God, this is the way *my* pictures are seen by my friends and peers! It's true. You simply don't get invited to showings of your own flicks.

Now, when it comes to a vote on whether to turn off a film in midstream, you may truly be hating the picture, but you empathize with the absent filmmakers, knowing how *you'd* feel if they did it to *your* picture. Still you don't want to be a spoilsport and insist on continuing to the end when so many others in the room don't want to. They might dislike you for that, you'd get to be unpopular on the Bel Air circuit. These are your friends and peers and colleagues, and you may even be working with some of them or will be working with some of them someday. So you go along with them and you hate yourself for doing it and you hate them for *potentially* disliking you if you didn't do it, and you think to yourself, You bastards, how dare you do that to my picture—and it isn't even your picture. Your picture is having that done to it in some *other* living room on the Bel Air circuit miles away.

All films shown on the circuit, however, don't get voted off the screen. In fact, some host-and-hostess teams would never dream of subjecting a picture, anyone's picture, to that kind of humiliation. It is purely a coincidence that such thoughtful hosts and hostesses just happen to have been unable to wangle any backup films for that particular evening.

And so the movie runs to its final fade-out, the living-room lights go up, the guests blink and rub their eyes and look around the room to read what they can find on each other's carefully expressionless faces. There is a long moment of wary silence, lasting perhaps five, maybe ten seconds. A series of studies carried out by a team led by Dr. Ernest Goodbody at Cal Tech has determined that, during these five to ten seconds, each person in the room undergoes sufficient hidden conflict to shorten his or her life span an average of four minutes, and that is for only one screening.

During those five to ten seconds, each person must make instant calculations, weigh the pluses and minuses of each option that is open, and formulate a point of view leading to a whole set of orderly and seemingly genuine behavior patterns. The human computer works swiftly. Unfortunately, nowhere in its private-screening calculations has it yet been programmed to consider the inner well-being of its human operator as a factor of any importance.

You *liked* the picture. What did the others think? How quickly can you prepare a defense against possible attacks? How far are you prepared to go? How much antagonism can this bunch take before they turn from disliking the picture to disliking *you?* In what current state is your security system? How much dislike can it tolerate? Hurry up. Your time's up. Have a Position on the picture, know exactly how many inches you can go out on the limb before a word is said in the room. So, you clear your throat and speak up: "Be right back. I've gotta go to the john."

Another time, you disliked the picture very much, but really very much. All the above still happens. With an added twist to your psyche: What will the host and hostess feel if you express yourself too honestly? After all, it's their movie you're attacking. They had nothing to do with the making of the film but they selected it. It's their offering for their invited guests. Be careful. They may speak out against the film they've shown, but don't let that lull you into total honesty. Get too vehement, too vituperative, too harshly critical, and without your even realizing it you will have offended them, as though you had criticized the dinner they had served, or the supper they had brought out after the screening. ("Are you daring to say that we have served a lousy movie in our own home to our own friends?") What you have done is, you have just honestly expressed yourself off their future invitation list, without understanding why it happened to you.

I know, you think you have an easy solution to the private-screening problem. Just don't say *anything* when the lights go up. Just listen. Listen a lot. Let the others do all the talking. Let them all hang themselves in one way or another with their clever critiques, their smart-ass put-downs, their well-put, extravagant praise, their lying enthusiasms. You'll just sit there sipping your highball, nibbling on your cheese, and nodding your head diagonally. It takes you a year before you realize why you don't get invited to the living rooms on the Bel Air circuit anymore.

"He never has an opinion. He just sits there and says nothing."

Perhaps the increasing incidence of screening sickness in the land accounts, in part, for the record-breaking grosses taken in by the nation's theaters during the past few years. Apparently never in history have so many people liked a picture too much at the wrong time, or disliked a picture too much at the wrong time, or maintained too much cautious silence too long on too many occasions, and thereby talked or not talked themselves right out of the comfortable living rooms of Bel Air into the wineless, cheeseless discomforts of America's movie houses.

Notwithstanding the fact that they'll live a helluva lot longer, it serves them good and right.

The Film Critic

It was morning in New York. Outside the bathroom window, on the streets of the city below, the only city in the world that meant anything really, the movers and shakers were moving and shaking their pale-skinned, slightly misshapen bodies through their hurried paces as they went about the business of making the world safe for elitism. Inside the bathroom, standing before the mirror above his sink, Herman Hauser, film critic beyond compare, strove desperately to accomplish something he had never quite succeeded in doing to his complete, or even partial, satisfaction. He was trying to give himself a close shave without actually looking at himself.

Though he used a safety razor when shaving, Hauser invariably cut his face severely in his attempts to keep his eyes directed on, say, his *chin only*, or on the skin covering his *jaw* below the right *ear*, or when he stared fixedly at his *upper lip only* as he drew the razor across the grim and severe slash of his mouth. He hated shaving. It was so impossible. It was so difficult to narrow his gaze down to such specific and confined areas while eliminating the unsightly bristles on his face and *still* avoid the twin disasters he feared most: bloodletting, and looking himself in the eye. As film critic for *Manhattan*, the weekly sophisticated slick magazine for the weakly sophisticated slicks, Herman Hauser would go to any lengths to avoid looking himself in the eye, for he loathed movies intensely, and was deeply ashamed to be earning his livelihood reviewing them.

At one time, in order to obviate the necessity of shaving, and risking accidentally looking himself in the eye, Hauser had even contemplated growing a beard, but became afraid of the possibility of winding up as reviewer for the *Village Voice*, or of being mistaken for one of several Italian-American film directors and having $20 million thrust upon him by a syndicate of former money market fund administrators operating out of Leavenworth penitentiary, and being forced to make a motion picture filled with violence. Hauser abhorred violence.

He also abhorred sex, romance, situation comedy, domestic drama, suspense thrillers, horror films, action-adventure melodramas, drawing room comedies, farce, Westerns, musicals, science fiction epics, historical dramas, film biographies, documentaries, industrial films, student films, recruitment films, animated full-length features, animated shorts, live-action shorts, political dramas, political comedies, fantasies, religious themes, pornography, animal pictures, movies about children, movies about child molesters, movies about man-eating plants, and movies about plant-eating men. Hauser just didn't like movies, which is why he had such a devil of a time shaving.

On several occasions, he had tried changing occupations, but each time, he had run into the same difficulty. There was, apparently, nothing else he knew how to do except review movies. He would haunt the employment agencies in the poorer neighborhoods on the Avenue of the Americas, and try desperately to secure work as a dishwasher, or as a meat packer, or as night cashier at Waldorf's Cafeteria. And always he would be told the same thing: You are underqualified. You hate movies? Go get a job as a film critic.

But I can make change at Waldorf's as well as anyone else, he would plead. Just give me the chance to prove it.

Whaddaya think this job is, mister, trashing Truffaut? Fracturing Friedkin? Excoriating Scorsese? Making change is *responsible work.*

And so, this morning, as he had for so many mornings in the past, Herman Hauser, in the bathroom of his apartment overlooking the streets on which the movers and shakers moved and shook, applied the bloody tip of his Cutstick to the many wounds on his face, an uncommon feat considering that his head was turned away from the mirror, and prepared to get dressed for the day's upcoming press screening. Donning a conservative navy-blue suit, a pale champagne shirt, and a small-figured maroon bow tie, Hauser set out for the coffee shop downstairs. He would have his breakfast there, and rehearse.

He liked the emptiness of the coffee shop at this late morning hour. His corner table was always there waiting for him. He sat with his back to the wall, facing the entrance, minimizing the chance of a sudden ambush or gangland-style rub out by some vengeful producer, director, or actor whose career he had ruined, or whose life he had wrecked, whichever came first. On the table before him, right next to the pepper and salt, sat the small can of Mace. He never went anywhere without it.

Now, while breakfasting on orange juice, bacon and eggs, toast and coffee, pausing only occasionally for deep, reflective thought, he studied the script he had prepared the night before for today's screening room adventure, using the studio synopsis of the film. Though he had his lines down cold, he always liked to do a final run-through at this time, so that his talk back to the screen would be perfect in its wording and faultless in its timing, and appear to be completely spontaneous to his appreciative colleagues.

With the baser side of his nature, Hauser treasured his two-ply reputation, and worked hard to maintain it. On the one hand, there were his acidulous, corrosive, devastating reviews, written with erudition and naked malice. His eastern readers reveled in his destructiveness, for it was an outlet for their own repressed hostility toward the fools on the western coast. In Hollywood the film colony went into transports of glee every time a Herman Hauser review appeared. Those who died a bloody death at his hands, those unfortunates who had worked on the film, were a mere handful compared to the thousands of others in the business who exulted in the public execution of their best friends, their competitors.

This was Hauser's chief and public claim to fame, and the cuts that he suffered in the bathroom each morning seemed to be small enough price to pay for the vast reputation that overshadowed the secret shame which sent him, so often, to the employment agencies of the Avenue of the Americas in search of a dish that would let him wash it, or a cafeteria cash register that would suffer his fingers to ring up eighty-five cents out of five dollars.

And in addition, there was this other and lesser-known reputation, one which Hauser regarded with the greatest pride of all. His skillful badinage with his fellow reviewers, as they sat in the darkened screening room on all sides of him, and the dazzlingly witty repartee he engaged in with the sound track of the film under observation made him the darling of his kind. No matter how dull the film, no matter how fine and intelligent it was, the reviewers' experience was inevitably enhanced by the flurry of carefully rehearsed witticisms which Hauser introduced into the dark and smoky air.

Studio executives, distributors, and publicity agents did nothing to inhibit Hauser's behavior at press screenings. Over the years, they discovered that his comportment, while it interfered with comprehension of the film's dialogue and continuity, actually induced good will into the hearts of the other critics, who left the screening room somehow *entertained*, no matter what had been up there on the screen. Many an intended critical denunciation came out softer, kinder, more mellow, thanks to Herman Hauser's jeering japes. Indeed, authorities in the field of movie reviewing have speculated that some of the newspaper, magazine, and network film critics with unusually long tenure were stayed in their desire to go on to other challenges only by their reluctance to give up the Herman Hauser experience.

All this Hauser reflected on as he sat sipping his second cup of coffee, and suffering from the wounds on his face. In many ways he had brought much happiness to the world. Why could he not dwell more upon that aspect of life, instead of thinking of those for whom he carried the can of Mace? What difference that he pretended to sit in impartial critical judgment of film work that he detested before he had even seen it? Should he not give himself credit for the ameliorating influence that his comic turns had on the cold-hearted among his colleagues? Was it really that grossly humiliating to know that one's professional existence was bound up with the work of people who lived for the most part in Southern California?

Hauser got up from the table, paid his check, joined the throngs on the busy street outside, and walked west toward the screening room.

He must learn not to be so hard on himself. He must learn

to accept himself. He must learn to see the *good* side of himself, not just the bad. All this he kept telling himself as he made his way westward toward the screening room. But the more he kept telling himself these things, the more he was aware of the terrible pains in his face. With each step he took, the cuts on his neck and his jaw and his chin and his upper lip seemed to grow worse and worse, and he wondered for how many more years he could go on enduring this punishment.

Suddenly he came to a stop and stood there staring at a sign in the window of a fast-food establishment: Counterman Wanted. His heart leaped. Tears came to his eyes. Taking one last look around him at the throngs on the streets of the only city in the world that mattered really, Herman Hauser went inside, gave a false name, lied about his background, and got the job, never to be heard of again.

He will be missed.

Advice to
the Lovelorn

In the belief that most of you who browse through books like this are engaged, one way or another, in the making of theatrical films and television productions, or are hoping and intending to *be* thus engaged, it seems to me that it would be worthwhile for you to know exactly why some people go to the movies these days, or don't go to the movies these days, and why some people stay home and watch television, or don't stay home and watch television.

I know all about the widely held assumption that it is the quality of your creative efforts and the shrewd commerciality of your thinking that are the crucial determinants in the success or failure of your achieving and holding on to an audience, and I don't for a moment mean to imply that such factors are not worthwhile and vitally important. But I would like, nevertheless, to lay before you some rather crude and inartistic observations that I have assembled, with the aid of a simple pocket calculator, several articles from *The Wall Street Journal*, and a few interviews with friends, that may throw additional light on this subject that is so dear to your self-interested little hearts.

I will start with Ira Moray, because he and his family and their entertainment-seeking habits are about as typical as those of anyone I happen to know. Ira said he would sue me if I used his name in this book, but the hell with him. Let him sue. I'm not saying anything that isn't true, or that will make the Moray family look any worse than or different from anyone else.

About ten days ago, Ira and his wife, Penny, and their two kids, Laurette, fourteen, and Adam, eleven, decided to go to a local movie together. Ira drove the Seville instead of the Porsche, because there were the four of them and they are rather large-bodied and it wouldn't have been too comfortable in the sports car, even though the ride to the theater from their home in Bel Air was only four and a half miles. Parking, which used to be half a buck, was $2.50. The tickets, because it was a neighborhood second-run Cinema I and II–type theater, were only $5.50 apiece. Adam and Laurette each bought a ten-cent Hershey bar for a dollar, Penny had a ten-cent glass of Pepsi for seventy-five cents, and Ira had nothing, for a quarter.

So far, it would appear that it cost Ira only $27.50 *going in*. But to that you have to add $1.35 for the gallon of unleaded gasoline used for the nine-mile round trip by the Seville (thirteen mpg in the city; twenty-three mpg on the highway) and $14.75 for depreciation on the car during the three hours the Morays were in the theater. Also, Laurette got so frightened when the head came up out of the grave and bit off the boy's arm in the last reel that she soiled her brand-new $100 Rive Droite dress, which Penny had bought for her on sale for only $400. And when Penny took the dress to the best dry cleaners in Beverly Hills, they accidentally ruined the garment, and the insurance company refused to pay damages because they said it was the fault of the fabric. Ira went to his lawyer with the thought of suing the distributor of the picture, but the lawyer told him it would cost too much money to go to court over something as inconsequential as a fourteen-year-old girl being rendered incontinent by a PG-rated movie, and charged him only $100 as a token fee for the advice.

About this time, little Adam started developing nightmares over some of the milder horror stuff in the picture, so Penny took him to a $90-an-hour child psychiatrist on Bedford Drive, who cured the boy in one session, which came to only $2 for each of the forty-five minutes.

Struck with these added expenses of $606.10, Ira went to his accountant and asked him if it was *possible* that it could have cost him $633.60 for one night at the movies.

"What was the running time of the picture?" the accountant asked.

"Three hours," Ira replied.

"How long was the drive to and from?"

"Twenty minutes each way," Ira said.

The accountant punched some buttons on his desk calculator with swiftness and dexterity.

"In the three hours and forty minutes that you were away," he said, "your house in Bel Air went up in value $4,100, meaning that your profit on the evening, before taxes but *including* my fee for this analysis, was $3,466."

"My God," Ira cried, "I should go to the movies every night."

"You certainly should," the accountant said. "It's like stealing money."

So there's Ira Moray for you. OK?

Now take this acquaintance of mine by the name of Lester Charnock. He said he couldn't care less whether I use his name or not, but his wife, Gloria, said don't you dare, so I'll call her Sylvia. The Charnocks never had any use for the movies. They used to boast that they hadn't been to one in years—a fact that was quite important to them because it was literally the only thing in their lives that they could boast about. They live in St. Louis, and it gets hot as hell in St. Louis in August, so naturally their apartment is air-conditioned. But like everything else in this world, their air conditioning broke down the middle of this past August, and in order to save their lives, they went to the nearest freezing movie theater, a classy first-run house whose right name I better not use.

"Never mind what's playing," Lester said to the girl at the box office. "If it's less than eighty degrees inside, I'll take two in the shade."

But the Charnocks were not accustomed, like some people are, to stepping out of the glare of the sweltering St. Louis sunshine into the pitch-black darkness of a movie house. So wouldn't you know? Lester, groping around in the dark, sat down right on top of a woman who was eating an ice-cream cone upside down. And when he shot forward with a shriek, he hit his face on the back of the head of the man sitting in front of the woman holding the inverted cone, breaking two front teeth and necessitating gold- and platinum-lined restorations, which Stanley N. Fogel, a prominent St. Louis dentist, assured him looked more real than the real thing.

"I should hope to smoke a herring they do," Charnock said when he got the bill for $1,500.

Mrs. Charnock didn't fare half as badly as her husband. In fact, she tells her friends, because she thinks it's funny, that she got into the movie that day for half fare. Meaning it cost only $680 in medical expenses for the sprained ankle, and

$75 to replace the six-inch spike-heel Joseph Magnins, which were ruined when her right spike got caught in a piece of totally masticated bubble gum on the floor of the theater and the left spike slid in an easterly direction on the melted remains of an Eskimo pie, causing Sylvia to do a split that had everything in it but the banana.

The Charnocks' lawyer was a damned good one, though not cheap, hitting them for 33⅓ percent of the hundred-grand settlement.

The Charnocks go to the movies all the time now, but so far they haven't made another dime out of it. They've become so accustomed to coming in out of the sunshine into the pitch-black darkness of the theater that nothing much happens anymore. And what's worse, they have absolutely nothing to boast about now.

So that's the Ira Morays for you, and that's the Lester Charnocks, too. Big moviegoers, and *really motivated*. Eventually, I'm sure, they'll wind up on the other side of the coin, because real estate can't appreciate *forever*, and accidents only happen when you don't want them to. Which will bring them inevitably—and brings *us* now—to television.

I give you Herbert Schlamm. Herbie is a guy I went to college with. He happens to be the most typical television watcher in the *world*. Forget Nielsen, take Schlamm, if you want to know what to make for television. For example, Herbie will not look at any program that does not have at least one commercial every four minutes. That's *four minutes*. You can have twelve Freddie Silvermans going for you, you're never going to come up with a clue like *that*.

Another. Herbie Schlamm likes ugly women on TV. Go back and read that again. I said *ugly*. Herbie believes that ugliness on TV makes the women in your life look beautiful, whereas gorgeous women on the tube make you bitter about your own lot in life. Herbie should know, because he's got a lot of lot in his life. Another thing, he insists that talk-show guests should be impossibly dull. He feels that the smart-talking ones make *you* feel leaden and stupid, and who wants that? You're dumb enough to begin with just *watching* a talk show.

I'm not sure any of the foregoing is going to be helpful to you in a practical way. It may all be a little too *specific*. So let me make a few generalizations, and wrap it up. People go out to the movies because they can't stand what's on television. And people stay home and watch television because they can't abide the kind of movies they seem to find in their local theaters. Therefore, if you start making different kinds of films, particularly better ones, television will lose its audience to the movies. And if the networks and independents start to vary their programs and put on noticeably higher-quality stuff, no one will leave home to go to a flick. The result, as you can see, will be a double disaster.

So, for God's sake, don't change a thing.

I'm Sorry,
These Seats
Are Taken

"Arthur, how about going to a movie tonight?"

"What, pay five bucks a ticket to sit in some lousy, littered, smelly theater and suffer through an hour of filmed commercials waiting for the feature to go on? It's a damned outrage, that's what it is, and I'm sick and tired of being the only one who ever says anything about it. How dare those theater owners sell me a ticket for all that money under the guise of offering me entertainment, a *movie*, the one on the marquee, and then once they've got me trapped in there, a helpless captive audience, they start boring me with filmed *advertisements*, *commercials*, selling me *products*, for the hawking of which they, the theater owners, receive money. Why should I have to pay them for the displeasure of watching their damned advertisements, huh, huh?"

"Well, aren't you always telling me that you buy *Playboy* and *Penthouse* because you like to look at the ads?"

"That's different!"

"I'll *bet* it is."

"And what *about* those movie houses? How about the filth on the floors? What excuse have those managers got for not cleaning the seats and the floors and the aisles between each showing? They strut around the lobby in their tuxedos and let *us* pay five bucks each to walk inside into their garbage dumps. Tuxedos, yet. I'll bet they're wearing dirty underwear underneath."

"You're disgusting, do you know that?"

"*They're* wearing dirty underwear, and *I'm disgusting?*"

"Do you want to go to a movie tonight or not?"

"*I'll* tell you why they don't clean up their theaters. It's because they need all their ushers and usherettes and assistant managers to work behind the candy counter at intermission time, raking in all that dough in exchange for the sugar-filled crap they foist on the youth of this country, kids whose food tastes and perfect teeth will never be the same again because they were unlucky enough to grow up with the moviegoing habit. If it weren't for the theater owners of America and their hired hands, the young people of this country would be thriving on fruits and vegetables and lean meats and fish and poultry and whole-grain breads and cereals. Instead, their teeth are stuck together with chocolate and caramel and marshmallow and raspberry *junk*, washed down with sugar-filled, artificially flavored poisons.

"And will you please tell me why a person can't see a movie without eating buttered popcorn by the quart? Let's forget the stink it makes for anyone sitting within ten yards. Let's not mention the sound of crunching jaws while *you're* trying to concentrate on the film. I want to know why all these obese unfortunates, who either have just *had* a meal or are *about* to have one when the picture ends, are filling themselves with popcorn. Don't answer me. I'll tell you why. They've been brainwashed into this nutritional hell by the operators of the nation's movie houses, those middlemen of our country's culture, who sell their audiences on dental cavities and fatness, first on the screen with commercials and then for real in the lobby.

"I asked a theater manager recently how the picture was doing, and he said: 'Terrific. Twelve hundred Krunchy bars and forty pounds of popcorn on opening day, and over the weekend we topped our old record by seven tanks of Poopsie.' I tell you, if they could figure out how to get their candy customers into the theaters without offering them a film, they'd do it, believe me. It would be good-bye motion-picture industry."

"Why are you telling all this to *me*, Arthur? Why don't you tell it to Ralph Nader?"

"Agh, he's too busy getting automobiles recalled, which is ridiculous to begin with. They should be recalling the *drivers*, not the cars. Cars don't have accidents. Drivers do. If I had my way, Nader would be having every movie-house manager and projectionist in the country recalled immediately."

"Oh, now it's the *projectionists*. What's wrong with *them?*"

"Everything. Either they run the sound too low, or they don't put enough light on the screen, or I'm hearing whatever *they're* hearing on their transistor radios up in the booth. I go to the head usher and say, I'd like to see the manager. I'm sorry, sir, he says, he just stepped out. Is anything wrong? Well, for one thing, the sound is too low, I can't hear the dialogue. That's strange, sir, he says. You're the only one who has complained. How can they complain? I say. Their teeth are stuck together.

"What else seems to be the problem, sir? There's not enough light on the screen. Look at how dark those faces are. They're supposed to be, sir, he says. This is a sequel to *Roots*. The hell it is, I say. It's a musical version of Noel Coward's *Hay Fever*, and that woman up there is lily-white. Next week, sir, Lily White is next week. No, no, no, that's Lily Tomlin. Look, let me speak to the projectionist. He's not in the booth, sir. Not in the *booth*? Where is he? He's over at Cinema Three, sir. Doing what? He's trying to locate a reel that's missing from Cinema Two. The audience is stomping, sir.

"Well, when he gets back to Cinema *One*, tell him to turn down his radio, will you? Radio? He doesn't play a radio up there, sir. He doesn't, huh? Then how come I know the Dodgers just scored three runs in the bottom of the seventh? You're the first one who's said that, sir. No, I'm not. Vin Scully just said it before me. But it's not even the baseball season any longer, sir. I know. That's how far behind the times your stupid projectionist is. Look, I've had enough of this. I'm not getting anywhere with you. I want my money back, or give me a rain check. I'm sorry, sir, you're too late. The movie has already gone five reels. It's in the record books as a legal showing. And *that*, my dear wife, is what's wrong with the projectionists *and* the ushers *and* the managers *and* the owners."

"What I like about you, Arthur, is that you never exaggerate. You never get intemperate. You're always so rational and fair-minded. Now, can I interest you in making us members of the *audience* tonight?"

"Audiences! *Those* slobs. They ruin every movie I go to. Some past, present, or future winner of the Writers Guild of America Laurel Award can have spent a year and a half working on the dialogue up there on the screen, but you can't hear it because all the Saturday-night smart-asses in the audience are trying to impress their dates with *their* dialogue. Why don't we go back to silent pictures, so that all the wise guys and their giggling girlfriends can be *heard?* And if you *say* anything to those guys, they're just as likely as not to climb over the seats and let you have a chocolate-stained, hot-buttered fist in your face."

"Isn't that how you lost that expensive pair of bifocals last year?"

"Agh, it was an old prescription anyway, and you should've seen the blood on the guy's hands afterward. That was no chocolate syrup, sister."

"I'm not your sister. I'm the wife who wants to go to the movies."

"OK, OK. Let's leave this lovely, comfortable living room and drive through the traffic and find some parking lot that charges only a paltry three dollars and walk the five blocks through the rain to that *pleasant* girl at the box office who may or may not get off the phone with her boyfriend long enough to take our ten dollars and allow us to stand outside in the rain in the line that has to wait out there in order to convince passersby that the picture is a smash-hit sellout, and then finally let's go inside into the frigid, overly air-conditioned, half-empty theater and sit down behind a girl who's wearing either a beehive hairdo or a Bella Abzug hat and a guy who is intent on doing to her what he should be doing to her on her living-room sofa instead of right in front of us, because all he's going to wind up with is the mouthful of popcorn she's already got stuffed in hers. . . ."

"You could always change your seat, you know."

"How can I move when the soles of my shoes are stuck to the floor with chewing gum? And it's no use trying to say anything to me because I can't hear you because seated on your left is a fat lady who is going to be spending the next two hours furtively trying to work the crackly, crinkly, *noisy* wrapper off a candy bar, and seated on my right is a man who is trying very hard to breathe through either his nose or his mouth but is never going to make it anyplace except on the very top of the Magic Mountain, and if he came here because he heard it was a Mann Theater, he ain't gonna find Thomas here, I'll tell you that. So what's playing tonight?"

"Let me see here in the paper. At the Valley, the show starts at eight, and the feature goes on at ten. Starts with Gleem toothpaste, then Revlon, with Ann-Margret playing a fingernail, then Trader Vic's, the Los Angeles *Times*, Hong Kong Air Tours, with Robert Goulet singing 'Just Give Me Sampan to Remember You By,' then Chrysler Imperial, Ramada Inn, Wonder Bread, 31 Flavors, Gillette Triple Edged Blades, Smiling Ed, the Used Car King, and . . ."

"What's the feature? What's the *movie*?"

"I don't know. They don't list it."

"OK. What's playing at the Ravioli?"

"It says here the world premiere of the 1984 Cadillac line. . . ."

"World premiere my foot. We already saw it. Don't you remember? We walked out during the Sedan de Villes."

"Yes, that's right. Wait a minute, here's one you'll probably like. Ruth Fleegle in Maidenform Bras, winner of last year's best-supporting Oscar. And on the same bill, Paul Newman in Champion Sparkplugs, Faye Dunaway in Sees Candies, Robert Morley and Peter Ustinov in Weight Watchers, and a musical version of Amtrak with a score by Jule Styne and Bob Merrill. Gene Shalit says: 'Amtrak will have you rolling in the aisles.' Sheila Benson says: 'You'll be sorry if you miss it.' And *Cahiers du Cinéma* says: 'There's been nothing like it since *The Covered Wagon.* Sounds good, Arthur."

"All right, all right, you win. Get the umbrellas and the heavy cardigans and the mufflers and the Energine and the cleaning rags and the Lysol and the Airwick spray and my brass knuckles, and let's go to the movies."

Close Encounters
of a Quibbling Kind

"But suppose they misconstrue my yearnings for answers," he said half-aloud. "Suppose they don't realize I really love it and admire it and respect it?"

"What are you doing?" she said. "Are you *talking* to yourself or something?"

He looked at her. "I want you to know that I'm going out there again tonight."

"Oh, no, you're not," she said.

"Yes, I am," he said.

She turned on him with harsh expression. "Why, dammit, *why?*"

"Because I have to see it all happen again. I have to see if I can begin to understand it. There has to be *some* explanation for all those things I *can't figure out.*"

"People are going to laugh at you," she cried. "They're

going to laugh at *me*. You're making a fool of yourself. How many times is it now?"

"Not counting the six times during the first version, the eleven times during the second edition, and the year on pay TV, *twelve*," he said. "And tonight will make thirteen."

"Well, don't be surprised if I'm not here when you get back!" And with that she stormed out.

And with that, he went out to the Place again, and stood there in the darkness surrounded by others like himself, waiting patiently to have it wash over them once more, powerless to resist the psychic urge that had been implanted in their unconscious minds, their faces marked by the telltale signs of previous exposure, some on the left side, some on the right, the same sticky smudgy residues of candy bars and popcorn.

And then at 10:30 P.M. they came, as they had on all those other nights, their powerful beams shining before them, and sang out: "All right, please stay close to the building and have your tickets ready as you enter through the lobby."

He tried to make his voice heard above the howling wind and the blowing sand, shouting to the interpreter, François Spielberg, who in turn shouted to Steven Lacombe, the architect of this mighty project: "Lacombe, tell me why you and all these other men are acting so *surprised* as you inspect the planes. You came here to Mexico with a list of serial numbers of the missing planes, did you not? Why all this visible astonishment as your men discover these are the missing planes? What did you think they were? And how come everyone acts so stunned when they open the cockpit doors and find no pilots inside? Did you expect there would be? Didn't anybody who first discovered the planes tell you *anything* about them? Answer me, Lacombe, stop hiding behind the beard of your interpreter. Why did you and the others react to the old Mexican's words as though this was news to you? 'The sun came up last night, and it sang to me,' he said. Was this the first time you heard about the Great Light and the Music in the Sky? If so, what brought you here? If not, why the phony overreactions? What is going on here? What is the purpose of this confusion you are creating? I have a great psychic need to know the answer. Speak to me, Steven Lacombe!"

The director of the project muttered into the ear of his interpreter, François Spielberg, and the bearded one cupped his hands to his mouth and shouted hoarsely: "It is as plain as the sand on your face!"

He heard his wife answering the telephone. "Oh, no," she cried out, "you can't do that to him, please. He is not that kind of person. All he did was—hello? . . . Hello? . . ."

He heard her hang up. Then she appeared in the doorway, white-faced, her cheeks damp with tears. "I can't believe it," she sobbed.

"What is it?" he said.

"That was your producer. You're fired."

"Fired?"

"He read in the trade papers about your seeing it twelve times. You're fired."

"That's strange, very strange," he mused."

"What's so strange? It makes sense to *me*. I warned you."

"No, you don't understand. You see, I know why *I* was fired just now. But I still don't know why *Roy Neary* was fired. What did he do exactly that got him fired? There must be some reason why Steven Lacombe wanted to keep me in mystery. He could have let me know the reason for Neary's discharge with four or five words of dialogue, but he didn't. *I must find out what is going on here.*"

"Oh, my God . . ."

"I'm going out there again tonight."

"No, you're not."

But he was already running to his car in the driveway, gunning the motor, and driving away with no automotive difficulties whatsoever, just as though the entire dashboard of his car and all the gauges *and* the windshield hadn't been blown to bits a few minutes earlier by some sort of encounter with aliens from another studio.

He found Lacombe and Spielberg in a small enclosure with the others. The men were all talking at the same time, and he knew this was deliberate, so that he would not be able to understand what was going on. But he made out Lacombe's voice saying: "They are replying to us with sets of numbers. What can they mean?" And then François Spielberg's voice was calling out above the hubbub: "Excuse me . . . excuse me . . ." until the men turned to him and fell silent, and then the bearded one spoke. "Gentlemen, before I became an interpreter I was a copy editor for *Variety,* and these numbers, these sets of figures, are simply the weekly grosses from major cities in the United States, and they are telling us that we have something here that is even more magnificent than we ever dreamed it could be. We are out in front of all the rest, all by ourselves. Gentlemen, the news is: *We are alone!*"

Immediately, the small enclosure was filled with the sound of cheering and thunderous applause.

"Just a second!" a voice cried out. "I have some questions to ask! Men, hear me out, I beg of you! *Listen to me!*"

The cheers stopped. The men turned to the intruder. Steven Lacombe stepped forward. "Wait a minute. Aren't you the same man who—"

"Yes, I am," he said. "The very same. And what I wish to know this time is as follows: When you traveled way the hell to Benares in India, why did you record the musical chant of a few thousand native extras?"

"The answer to that is obvious," Lacombe replied. "The men were chanting the sounds they had heard from the sky."

"Right," said the intruder. "So, Steve, baby, suppose you tell me why, knowing what you had already been told which brought you hurrying to Benares, tell me *why* you and Spielberg and the rest of you big-time international scientist types climbed to the top of a hill, looked down at those thousands of Indian extras, and shouted: 'And where did the sounds come from?'"

Steven Lacombe's eyes lit up. "Didn't you see that great shot of three thousand index fingers coming up from below the frame onto the screen in one giant, breathtaking thrust pointing to the heavens?"

"Of course, I saw it, and it was a great shot, but what did it mean?"

"Up yours!" roared Lacombe.

They sat at the dining room table, his querulous wife and his uncomprehending children, and they looked at him with condescending pity. Their lips quivered, and the tears came to their eyes. He was doing it again. This time it was chopped liver. He was spooning gobs of chopped liver onto his plate and then shaping it with his hands, molding the mass into what looked vaguely like a script with holes in it, and then his fingers would thrust little dabs of liver into the holes as though he were trying to fill the holes without destroying the overall illusionary shape of the sculpture.

He pointed at the hand-molded chopped liver on his plate. "This means something. . . . This is important."

"You're darned right it is. It took me all afternoon to make it. Eat it!"

How could he explain to her, to anybody, what he was feeling, when he couldn't even explain it to himself, this irresistible urge to fill the holes in a script made of chopped liver? He had no way of knowing that all over America men and women who had Seen It and Heard It were acting out the same obsessive ritual.

And suppose he had known? Would it have helped him any to ask of them, "Who are those astronauts in the red uniforms, and why are they being sent to Devils Head, Wyoming? Which alien from another studio communicated with which international scientist in which scene and in what language or in what key and on whose alto sax, to give us folks here on little old earth *any reason whatsoever* to believe that a spaceship was coming down to take some of our people aboard? And toward the end, when a clergyman blesses the astronauts and then a few moments later they file off to go bravely aboard the waiting ship, *who* invited them, and *when?* And can any of you please whistle or hum the invitation to me, because *I* was stupidly assuming that what the magnificent final sequences of this truly monumental film were depicting was the mutual efforts of an international team of earth scientists and a group of extraterrestrial beings to work out a means of communicating with each other through tonal combinations and variations? Did I miss some crucial moment when the key to two-way understanding was discovered? Is that why I was so confused by the behavior of the scientists who acted as though they knew what was going on even though I was given no clues?"

No, he could have asked these questions of the others like himself, but the answers would have been more questions from *them*, niggling little questions like: "Why did Roy Neary buy *two* gas masks when he was all alone? How did he know that he would find Gillian if he started searching for her on a train taking evacuees *away* from the 'contaminated' area? What happened to the live birds in Roy's cage, who suddenly were seen lying on their backs, feet in the air, when there was no lethal gas in the area?"

Steven Lacombe, gazing into the blinding white light pouring from the great mothership before him, felt a nudge in his ribs. "Here he comes," François Spielberg muttered to him.

Lacombe turned and frowned as he saw the intruder approaching with that quizzical, questioning expression on his face.

"At a time like this?" Lacombe cried.

"Yes," he said quietly.

"*Why?*"

"Because there is so much that I do not understand, so much that I have to know."

Lacombe leaned close to Spielberg and spoke to him in French in a low voice. Spielberg nodded with understanding, then clapped his hands. In a twinkling, a young white-coated aide came over to them, and Spielberg said to him: "Have this man outfitted immediately in a red suit."

The white-coated aide's eyes widened. "You mean—?"

"Yes," Lacombe broke in quickly. "He means."

"Thank you, Steven, thank you," the intruder called out, as the aide led him away, asking, "Have you ever had measles, smallpox, or an unsuccessful psychoanalysis?"

Lacombe turned now and gazed down with love and awe at the alien being from the mothership who had moved up to stand before him, bathed in a shining mist. They exchanged several hand signs. Lacombe nodded. The being smiled, then turned and glided toward the ramp and up into the incandescent glow.

The figure in the red suit came scampering up in the rear,

the last one to go aboard, turning for one last moment to look back and silently mouth the words "Thank you, Steven, thank you."

Then the opening started to close, the blinding white light disappeared, and the giant starship took off into the night sky swiftly, as though trying to escape the obliteration that would befall it when the first credit of the end title came on the screen.

The two men gazed up at the vanishing spacecraft.

"What did you say to him, Steven?"

"*Him*, François?"

"*Her*, then. Whatever. What did you say with your hands?"

"That was an Extra-Terrestrial Being . . ."

"And what did you say to the Being, Steven?"

"Wait till they see *Raiders*, I said . . ."

"The Oakland Raiders?"

"Wait till they see *E.T.*"

"Eddie Travolta?"

"We'll show them, won't we, E.T.?"

And oh, how magnificently he did show us all . . .

"They'll want to eat their words," he concluded. "Especially these."

Mmmmm . . . *Delicious*. . . .

Will somebody pass the mustard please?

On the Importance of
Relative Importances

This was his first time out as a film director, and my first time out as a producer, and that was why we were having dinner together. He had had unparalleled, dazzling success directing in the theater: *Barefoot in the Park, Luv, The Odd Couple.* Extravagantly laudatory reviews, Tony Awards, standing ovations in Sardi's were the rule of the day for him. He could do no wrong, rarely did, and rarely has since. That night after dinner, as we stepped out of La Scala restaurant in Beverly Hills and waited at the curb for our cars, I said to him, "How does it feel, Mike, all this glorious glory, the cheers of the multitudes? It must be an incredibly satisfying experience."

"The only feedback that ever meant anything to me," he said, "the only reaction that I agreed with, that made any sense at all to me, was *Newsweek's* review of *The Odd Couple.*"

"Really? What did it say?"

He looked at me with pale blue eyes. "They didn't like it," he said.

A year later, the film we had made together, *Who's Afraid of Virginia Woolf?*, opened nationwide to the kind of thrilling notices and clamoring lines at the box office that one dreams about but so seldom realizes. For Mike Nichols in particular, the praise was so unstinting that even he could not ignore the fact that his first effort as a film director was a smashing personal success. I rushed over to his penthouse apartment on West Eighty-first Street in Manhattan with a large manila envelope packed with tear sheets of reviews from all over the country, and we spread them out on the sofa in his living room and read them aloud to each other, whooping and shouting and drinking and backpounding. . . .

"Listen to *this*. . . . No, listen to *this*. . . . Wait a minute, you think *that's* something, listen to *this*. . . . Wow, here's one that says. . . . Mike, here's one that's absolutely *unbelievable*. . . . My *God*, listen to *this!*" Elation? Hysteria? Like you never heard in your life. Chicago . . . Philadelphia . . . New York . . . Atlanta . . . Pittsburgh . . . St. Louis . . . Rave after rave after rave . . .

"Isn't this *wonderful?*" I cried.

The smile disappeared from his face. "Yes, Ernie," he said, with utter sincerity, "but we still have to die someday, don't we?"

Alfred Hitchcock must have heard something in my voice. "Stay where you are," he said. "I'll be right there."

I hung up and sat at my desk in my office at MGM, sat there with my head in my hands. That way, I wouldn't have to look at the blank piece of paper in my typewriter, with the

title *North by Northwest* in the upper-left-hand corner and
the page number, 126, in the upper right. It must have been
just as serious as I had feared it was. Hitch was leaving his
office at the other end of the building and coming to mine.

When he had settled in the leather club chair facing me,
he said, "All right, what seems to be the trouble?"

The words literally poured out of me (which is more than I
could say for my typewriter): "I don't know what to do, I
should have told you sooner, but each day I thought there'd
be a breakthrough, I haven't written a single word in two
weeks, there's no third act and this is only the first draft and
there's still no third act because I'm stuck, I haven't the faint-
est idea what to write next, and Bob Boyle is building sets and
Helen Rose is designing thousand-dollar dresses for Eva
Marie Saint and Cary Grant goes on salary next week at five
thousand dollars a *day* and you've got a starting date, you're
signing actors every five minutes, the studio thinks I've
finished the script and here I am sitting with no third act, no
idea where the story goes, who does what to whom next, for
two weeks now not a single word and he's gonna be getting
five thousand dollars a *day* while I sit here not knowing what
comes next, it's disaster, Hitch, it's sheer and total disaster!"

He extended his hands, palms upraised, and smiled. "Ernie," he said, speaking to a small child, "it's only a movie."

The following spring, I paced the carpet of another office
at another studio on another picture. It was late in the afternoon, and I couldn't *stand* it any longer. Almost twenty-four
hours ago, *North by Northwest* had had its first preview in
Santa Barbara, and not a soul had called me afterward, not
last night, not all this day. I hadn't had the guts to go to the
preview myself, but everyone else had gone, and not one of
them had called me, not Hitch, not Peggy Robertson, not
Bob Boyle, not my agent Edd Henry. Santa Barbara had

been a catastrophe, and I couldn't stand it any longer, I had to flee from my office and get in the car and drive somewhere, anywhere, to get away from the realization that calamity had overtaken us.

The telephone rang. My secretary buzzed me. "It's Cary Grant," she said.

"Cary Grant!"

"Shall I put him on?"

"No, no, tell him I've left for the day."

"But I already told him you were in."

"Oh, God . . . put him on."

I braced myself.

"Ernie!"

"Yes, Cary . . ."

"Wasn't it . . . *marvelous?*"

"Wasn't *what* marvelous?"

"Santa Barbara. Last night. Weren't you there?"

"No."

"Oh, Ernie, you missed the most fantastic preview I've ever been to in my whole life. You never *heard* such audience reaction. They laughed, they gasped, they cheered, and the *cards*—you should *see* those cards. I can't *begin* to describe what an exciting night it was, and I'm calling just to tell you how thrilled I am for you, for all of us. . . ."

When he was through and I had thanked him and said good-bye to him, I told my secretary to get my agent on the phone immediately.

"Hello, Edd?"

"Yes," he said.

"I hear the preview went great last night."

"That's right," he said. "It did."

"Were you there?"

"Of course, I was there. I told you I'd be there."

"How come you didn't call me last night, or sometime today?"

"What for?" he said.

"To tell me how the preview went," I said. "To tell me what a terrific preview my picture had last night."

"Let's get to something really important," he said. "How's the new script coming?"

Sweet Smell of Success had a starting date, and here I was struggling to write a scene that defiantly refused to be written. One of the executives of the film company stepped into my office. His face wore a worried expression. "What's that in your typewriter?" he said.

"The screenplay. The *unfinished* screenplay," I said bitterly.

"Take it out," he said, and handed me a blank piece of paper. "Put this in your typewriter instead."

"I've *got* to lick this scene," I protested. "It's absolutely *essential*."

He pointed to my typewriter. I did as I was told.

"You remember yesterday when we interviewed Roxanne?" he said (but used her *real* name). "You remember how we all agreed that she's the only one for the role?"

"Of course, I remember. How could I forget?" I said. "She's going to be fabulous. Have you signed her yet?"

He looked away from me. "Before she left here yesterday, I made a date with her and took her out to dinner last night, and then we went to her apartment afterward, and it was beautiful, Ernie . . . *it* . . . *was* . . . *beautiful*. . . ."

"Gee, how did you manage to swing *that?*" I asked.

"Simple," he said. "I told her I was in love with her."

"You're terrific," I said. "You'll do anything for the good of the picture, won't you?"

"Well, hell." He shrugged modestly. "We all know how vital it is that she says yes to that role."

I gestured toward the blank piece of paper in my typewriter. "So what do you want from *me?*"

"You're going to have to compose the note," he said.

"What note?"

"The one that's going with the flowers."

"What flowers?"

"The three dozen roses I've gotta send her right away."

"Three dozen roses? Why?"

"Because when I left her apartment in the middle of the night, I ran into the girl who lives next door to her walking her dog, and a few minutes later Roxanne woke up and caught us in bed together—"

"No!"

"Yes," he said dejectedly, "and she became hysterical and sobbed bitterly and swore that she would never, never talk to me ever again, so there goes the picture, Ernie, unless *you* come up with the right words on that piece of paper."

I looked at him. "Do you mind leaving me alone now?"

"Good luck," he said gloomily. "God, how I hope you're as good a writer as the idiots in this town say you are."

I came up with the right words, all right. The note was a big hit. Roxanne played the role in the picture, and she was sensational.

But I never did lick that scene in the screenplay.

I don't know how Billy Wilder felt deep down. I know *I* was scared stiff. He was going to start shooting *Sabrina* with an unfinished script. By day he'd be on the set directing. At night the two of us would be pacing the floors of his living room and den, trying to stay ahead, or at least stay even. At last there came a three-day break in the schedule to allow the company to travel to New York for location shooting.

"You and I will take the train," Billy announced to me. "For two and a half days we will be able to work without interruption. *Perfecto.*"

And so I boarded the *Super Chief* at Los Angeles with high hopes, six boxes of freshly sharpened pencils, and a dozen legal-size yellow pads. "This should do the trick," I said eagerly.

"My dear boy," Billy said, "we are only going to finish a screenplay. We are not going to write *Crime and Punishment.*"

As soon as the train had pulled out of Union Station, I entered Billy's compartment with pad and pencil at the ready, only to find him standing, face aglow, looking down at a porcelain dish containing one pound of fresh beluga Malossal caviar packed in shaved ice.

"Just look at it," he cried. "Did you ever see such magnificence? It's a gift from Swifty Lazar."

Just then, the porter he had summoned appeared in the doorway. Billy handed him the treasure, saying, "Would you please take this to the dining car and prepare it for immediate attack?"

I sat down and opened my pad.

"Come," Billy said. "Follow me."

"I thought we were going to work," I said feebly.

"We *are*," he said, "on Swifty's caviar."

"But, Billy . . ."

"Come," he said, and led me through the swaying train to the dining car, and sat me down at the table where the mountain of caviar loomed ceilingward, waiting.

"But, Billy," I said, "I don't like caviar."

"Stop talking nonsense," he said. "Dip in."

"But, Billy, I don't *eat* caviar. I never have. I hate it."

He looked at me in dismay and swallowed about forty dollars' worth. "What did you say?"

"I said, I *don't . . . eat . . . caviar.* I *despise* the stuff."

"Oh, my God," he groaned.

For three nights and two days (with a few hours here and there for sleep) we sat facing each other in his compartment, as first the *Super Chief* and then the *Twentieth Century Limited* bore us across the continent. For three nights and two days we stared out of the windows at the passing countryside, or we stared at each other, and both views were equally uninteresting to us. And not once in those three nights and two days did our lips move in creative speech, nor did my pencil move either, and here we were now approaching Grand Central Station in New York.

"Billy," I said, "do you realize we haven't written one word?"

He looked at me with a mixture of scorn and pity. "What am I, a genius?" he said. "How do you expect me to work with a man who refuses to eat caviar?"

Shooting was over.

He saw me at the typewriter in his den, pounding away.

"What the hell are you writing?" he said.

"The final scene in the picture," I said, "where Bogie gets Audrey."

"But I already shot it yesterday. It's on celluloid."

"I know," I said. "But it isn't on paper yet. *That's important.*"

Shop Talk

Pardon me, I'm thinking. . . .

These pieces don't write themselves, you know. They don't just sort of *happen*. There's a certain amount of *thought* involved before anything gets put down on paper, eventually to wind up on the printed page.

Sometimes, thinking doesn't do a damned bit of good. Like right now, for example.

What to write about? That is always the question. I don't really like to let you in on this phase of the operation. The theory is, What you don't know can't hurt me. But I've decided to change all that now. Come on with me on a studio tour. Climb aboard and see how movies are made. Well, not movies exactly, but words *about* them. . . .

OK, let's see, what've we got, what've we got? Madam President . . . the First Lady . . . beautiful young woman heading a major studio. . . . Sounds like a premise, doesn't it? . . . Fashion shows in the commissary? . . . Office of the

President now referred to as the Makeup Department? . . .
Hand kissing replaces the other kind of kissing at the studio?
. . . Unh-unh. No good. No way of doing it without sounding like the worst kind of male chauvinist. And it's a one-joke
joke all the way. Pointless, too. Why *shouldn't* a beautiful
young woman be president of a major film company? Why
must it always be a man? Why should *we* always have to do
it? Why should *they* always get to sleep late and putter
around in the garden and have lunch with the other girls at
the Bistro and then go buy out Giorgio's and Neiman-Marcus while *we* struggle with ICM and the Morris agency all
day? It's about time. They want equal rights? *Give* it to them.
Let them *be* presidents of major studios. Let them see what
it's *like*. One thing for sure, I'm not going to write about it. I
don't even want to think about it. It's too cruel. . . .

So what's it going to be? How about doing another one on
film critics? . . . Film critics? . . . That's right, film critics. . . . Why do you keep coming up with *that* one all the
time? . . . Why do *you* keep turning pale at the mere
mention of them? . . . Because I know I'll say something
they'll regret for the rest of their lives. . . . Don't you mean
something *you'll* regret for the rest of *your* life? . . . Skip it,
will you please? Just thinking about them makes me ill. . . .

How about the greening of Hollywood, the youth kick, the
new breed of studio executives? You know, the Little Red
Schoolhouse on the lot, so they can take meetings and get
their diplomas at the same time? You could really go to town
on that. . . . What is this "go-to-town" business? Do I have
to put the knock on everything? Isn't it possible that there is
much to be said in *favor* of youth in the executive suites of
the studios? . . . Well, if there is, why not say it then?
There's your piece. . . . Piece? Not a whole piece. Maybe a
couple of paragraphs. Or one paragraph. Actually a *sentence*.
Which could be reduced to one word. . . . OK, at least

you've got a *word*. . . . No, I don't. I could never use a word like that in a book like this. . . .

Trends . . . trends. . . . Have we got any new trends going for us in the world of films? Is outer space still in? Or is outer space out? . . . I think it's on its *way* out. The question is, how far out? There's a hell of a difference between being way out and far out, but I don't know what it is. And if outer space is out, what's in? Can intimate personal drama be called inner space? I guess I can call it anything I want. OK, so we now have inner space being in. But what happens if we start dealing with intimate personal drama that takes place in *outer* space? *Then* where are we? I don't know, and frankly I don't care. I'm still stuck with the problem of *this* space. . . .

Book reviews. Not actual books. Fantasy stuff. That might do it. . . . *Writer's Block* by Neil Simon . . . *Open-Heart Surgery Self-Taught* by Bob Fosse. . . . Keep going, keep going, you haven't run out of bad taste *yet*. . . . Movie sequels might be better than books. . . . *Kramer vs. Kramer in the U.S. Circuit Court of Appeals* . . . *Being There 2 (The Making of the President)* . . . *11*. . . . Enough. Forget it. I'd rather do a straight piece like "Will *Apocalypse Now* in Dolby Sound Bring Back Silent Films?" . . . Well, will it? . . . I doubt it. Maybe audiences will *think* they're seeing silent films because they can't *hear* anymore, but that's all. A thought just occurred to me, though it's not worth a piece: Why did I actually feel and believe that Marlon Brando had more heads on his front lawn than Bo Derek had beads on her head, and what, if anything, does this tell us about the differences in Coppola's use of his cinematographer and Blake Edwards' use of his hairdresser? Let the French cinema buffs get hold of that one and they'll *never* let go.

You know what? I think it's happening to you again. . . .

You're right, I can feel it. I'm lapsing into that delusional state in which I become convinced that movies are something that should be seen and not read about. Sorry, Andrew; sorry, Stephen; sorry, Pauline. When I'm in this mental condition, the sad truth for me is that nothing anyone writes about a film will ever change that film for better or for worse, nor will the words influence to any significant degree the filmmaker's next picture, or the next. All things taken into account, few filmmakers ever profit from criticism, just as, all things taken into accounting procedures, few of them ever profit from their pictures.

If writing about pictures becomes an empty exercise, what's left for the writer on films to write about? Well, there are always the men and women and children who *make* the pictures. You can try to analyze them, understand them, explain them, idolize them, trivialize them, revere them, kick them around a little, but it all becomes so meaningless. The words they say to you and the words you write about them are of no importance. Only the picture they put on the screen counts, and it's *everything*. Therefore, writers, directors, producers, actors, and all the rest of you, be quiet, will you, especially around journalists, and get to work. . . .

Come on, there must be *something* going on in the movie industry that's worth zinging. . . . I'm sure there *is*, but I've probably zinged it already. I can't go on zinging indiscriminately. I'll get thrown out of Southern California. I'm liable to find myself Zingin' in the Rain. . . . There, that's one. Musical chairs at the studios. . . . No, that's old hat. Anyway, you can't do it in a book. By the time it rolls off the presses, you're as obsolete as yesterday's trade papers. What else have you got for sale? . . . Well, you might do something on that celebrated playwright's alleged remark that "there are only seventy-eight interesting people in Los Angeles, and seventy-six of them play the trombone in *The Mu-*

sic Man." . . . No, I don't believe he ever said that. . . .
How do you know? . . . I know. Because he wouldn't have
said it. It would be playing at the Forty-sixth Street Theatre
in New York right now. . . .

I *got* it. . . .
What?
Do an about-face, become an apologist for the film community, for all of Southern California. Maybe you could get
the East Coast to *forgive* us. . . . Forgive us for what? Apologize for what? . . . Oh, *you* know, for all the wonderful films
and television shows we create that are seen all over the
world, for the magnificent climate, the gorgeous, high-spir-
ited women of style and talent, for the creative, hardworking
men and the wide-open freeways and the beautiful homes
and dazzling shops and exciting ball clubs, and for the swim-
ming pools and tennis courts and beaches and marinas and
great restaurants and desert resorts and ski resorts . . . apologize for *everything*. . . .

What? After all these years of successful lying to keep them
from coming out here? I should help them discover the
truth? Are you crazy?

The New Hollywood

Harry Farber has been a movie producer since you were in bloomers and I was in short pants. He has had more hits than Stan Musial; his flops are now classics, and he has won the Thalberg award only twice only because they don't give it to you three times. It has been said by some—and I believe it— that what Harry Farber *doesn't* know about making pictures you can stick in your left ear and still have twenty-twenty hearing.

One day, along came the New Hollywood.

Harry didn't even blink.

He knew, like he knew the back of his deal-signing hand, that the days of a studio putting up the dough to buy him properties, and the small change to buy him screenwriters, and the mint to get him directors, were gone forever. With his own money, of which he has beaucoup, Harry, being a shrewd cookie, wouldn't take a ninety-day option on *bupkes*. So he did what had to be done—he found himself a backer.

Sheldon Vanderbilt was a manufacturer of paper boxes. For a hobby, he collected money. At the time, he was worth ten million, and counting. He happened to have a couple of personal problems. Paper boxes and his wife, to him, were not sexy. And two, his money attracted annual downpours from the Internal Rainfall Service. He needed a shelter badly. So Harry Farber gave him an umbrella and a pair of rubbers, introduced him to a waterproof young actress, and shook hands on a sixty-forty partnership, meaning, Harry would have his hand in Sheldon's pocket sixty percent of the time, and for the other forty percent, Sheldon would be worrying that his wife would find out about the young actress, and kill him in his sleep.

New Hollywood, Shmew Hollywood. With Vanderbilt's bankroll behind him, Harry Farber, as a picture maker, was now as hot as a twenty-two-year-old pistol with a beard on it and a degree from USC cinema school. For three-quarters of a mil, he snapped up Herman Faulkner's latest novel in manuscript form before anyone else could even steal a Xerox copy of it, and promptly set it up at Universal, with Bill Feitelbaum doing the screenplay for a hundred and a half. Next, he flew to Boston, caught Max Sherwood's new drawing-room comedy on its way to Broadway, outbid Columbia's offer of a million by two hundred grand, and put it into work as a Paramount project with the playwright doing the adaptation. And loitering in the men's room at UCLA, Farber caught a film student scribbling a great movie idea on a urinal wall, optioned it for a scant ten thousand against a hundred, and set the kid up at Warners in Burbank.

"How do you like *that*?" Farber said to Vanderbilt. "We've got projects going at Universal, Paramount, and Warners for only two million peanuts."

"How long has *this* been going on?" cried the delighted paper-box manufacturer.

"It's the New Hollywood," Harry Farber exclaimed.

"Now what about Fox and Columbia and Filmways and The Ladd Company?" Vanderbilt asked, using words he had picked up when the young actress talked in her sleep.

"Gimme time," Farber said. "It's been only three days."

Within two weeks, he had a young writer (sixteen) working on an original at MGM/UA, a middle-aged novelist (twenty-eight) screenplaying his own unpublished novel at Twentieth, and a dark-eyed brunet writer-director named Sparrow Nightingale (nineteen) prepping a picture under the parasol of Zanuck/Brown. All of this for a mere four hundred Gs more. If Farber had any problem at all, it was how to remember the names of all the secretaries in all his offices as he bicycled from Universal City to Hollywood to Culver City to Burbank to Beverly Hills to Century City and back again.

The months rolled by smoothly. The scripters scripted. Harry Farber bicycled. Sheldon Vanderbilt made paper boxes. The young actress performed. The New Hollywood kept getting newer. And six Farber-Vanderbilt productions moved inexorably toward the screen.

The first little ripple in the still waters came on Marathon Street. Before the screenplay was even half completed, Paramount took a look at Max Sherwood's comedy, now on Broadway, counted the laughs on the fingers of one hand, called Harry Farber in, and said, "We've decided to change our minds. You're in turnaround."

"No sweat," Farber told Sheldon Vanderbilt. "It's the New Hollywood. I'll simply take it to Columbia."

Which he did, that day, and they took it over immediately, with enthusiasm.

Next, Universal turned thumbs down on Bill Feitelbaum's screenplay of the Herman Faulkner novel, and they didn't like two hundred thousand dollars' worth of rewrites by the

Hatchetts either, so Farber took the project to The Ladd Company, which snapped it up.

Then, the UCLA film student who had scribbled ten thousand dollars' worth of graffiti on a urinal wall failed to get to the end of his first-draft screenplay at Warners. Before Harry Farber's option on the idea expired, the kid did, from an overdose of mescaline.

Farber shrugged. "We'll write it off."

"Against what?" Sheldon Vanderbilt inquired.

"Future profits," said Farber.

About this time, a sharpie named Sartor Santoni, armed with a new kind of microcomputer, waltzed up to the tables at MGM's Grand Hotel in Vegas and took them for seven million dollars. Out of anger more than anything else, MGM/UA said, "We pass," to Farber's now completed original. Twentieth, on the other hand, gave no reason at all for turning cold on the middle-aged novelist's screenplay of his unpublished novel. So Farber set them both up at Filmways. And when Zanuck/Brown's parasol closed on Sparrow Nightingale, Farber took the dark-eyed writer-director over to Paramount.

"How are we doing?" Sheldon Vanderbilt asked his partner.

"Terrific," Farber replied. "We've got one going at Columbia, one at The Ladd Company, two at Filmways, and one at Paramount. Only thing is, I need a new bicycle."

Vanderbilt was no piker. Farber bought a ten-speed Schwinn. He also bought, in manuscript form, a first novel by his shoe repairman, and an original screenplay by a *Time* magazine movie critic. The first he set up at MGM/UA, and the second at Warners. (Twentieth had no interest in the Schwinn.)

The *Hollywood Reporter* came out with a front-page story

on Farber-Vanderbilt, and why not? They had seven pictures in production, didn't they?

Variety coined the term "mini major."

Then came the latest in the wave of management changes. Orion went to Filmways. Filmways went to Columbia. Columbia went to lunch. Twentieth's new management team took over Ma Maison. Zanuck/Brown went fishing. Paramount's production chief went independent. The Ladd Company took over Universal. Universal's Young Turks took over Warners. Warners' troika stepped in at Fox. MGM/UA's chairman went into hotel management. Allan Carr's tailor became president of Paramount. A chorus boy in *Grease II* became the new head of Columbia. The special effects team of *Star Trek II* took over MGM/UA. And all of a sudden, Harry Farber had seven projects in turnaround.

"Pas de problème," he assured Sheldon Vanderbilt. "All I do now is set up our entire slate with Sir Lew Grade."

But try as he might, he could not reach Sir Lew. It turned out the man was at the bottom of the sea, still trying to raise the *Titanic*.

"Simple," Harry Farber said. "We'll get *Canadian* financing."

"Really?" said Sheldon Vanderbilt.

"Sure," said Farber. "All it means is that we have to use Canadian actors, Canadian directors, Canadian cameramen, Canadian editors, Canadian makeup men, Canadian wardrobe mistresses, Canadian propmen, and Canadian limousine drivers, and shoot the pictures in Canada."

"But what about our Manhattan locales?" Vanderbilt asked in all innocence.

"Obviously you haven't seen Toronto," Farber said.

"What about our Acapulco picture?"

"Wait'll you see Montreal."

"And our two Vietnam epics . . ."

"Vancouver starts with a V, doesn't it?"

Harry Farber flew to Toronto and huddled with all the right people. But they gave him all the wrong answers. The hitch was, every Canadian actor, director, cameraman, editor, makeup man, wardrobe mistress, propman, and limousine driver was already tied up working on American films, and would be for the next eleven years.

"Worry not your pretty little rich little head," Harry Farber said to Sheldon Vanderbilt.

"Why should I worry," the paper-box manufacturer replied, "when I know I'm in such good hands?"

"Thank you, Sheldon," said Farber.

"There isn't a day goes by," said Vanderbilt, "that I don't ask myself: How long has *this* been going on?"

"It's the New Hollywood, Sheldon," said Farber. "You just gotta learn to swing with it."

"I'm learning, I'm learning," said Sheldon Vanderbilt. "So where do we swing next?"

Farber smiled shrewdly. "Coproduction deals," he said. "You'll love it."

The first one was a classic—a joint Italo-Franco-Portuguese-Spanish-Liechtenstein venture, with Farber-Vanderbilt giving away only U.S. and Canada, the U.K., Asia, Africa, Europe, the Middle East, Mexico, Latin America, and South America, splitting the rest of the world 20-20-20-20-20.

"We get only twenty?" Sheldon Vanderbilt inquired.

"If you want to put up another two million, Sheldon, I may be able to elbow Liechtenstein out of the deal," said Farber.

"No," said Vanderbilt, "I wouldn't do a thing like that to a little country like Liechtenstein."

Farber next set up the Max Sherwood drawing-room comedy as a joint venture between a Japanese syndicate and a Third World combine of seven newly formed African republics. The only stipulations were that the director would have to be Japanese, eighty-five percent of the cast would have to be African, and all shooting would have to be done in Chad, necessitating a certain amount of rewriting by Max Sherwood. The playwright-turned-screenwriter demurred in rather noisy and obscene fashion, so a Philippine distributor was cut in for a piece of the action, and in turn provided a rewrite man fresh out of a Manila film school.

"The beauty of this deal," Harry Farber explained to Sheldon Vanderbilt, "is that *you* have to put up only seven hundred and fifty thousand dollars, and *we* get all of the western Carolines."

"Do you really think the western Carolines are going to go for a Max Sherwood comedy?" Vanderbilt asked.

Farber nudged his backer with a meaningful elbow and grinned slyly. "Do you really think this picture is going to be a Max Sherwood comedy after *these* turkeys get through with it?"

He had no trouble at all setting up Bill Feitelbaum's adaptation of the Herman Faulkner novel as a Bavarian Films production, to be shot entirely in Munich and released as a beer commercial on German television. After that, it would be edited down to a shorter version and released as a theatrical film, with subtitles, throughout Lapland.

At first there were some difficulties with the Acapulco film project, and with the two Vietnam epics, when a Greco-Icelandic syndicate insisted that all three were worth doing only as musicals. Rather than compromise his artistic integrity, and Sheldon Vanderbilt's, Harry Farber turned down the deal and took the projects to Katmandu Classics, Ltd., in Nepal, where financing was set up with frozen funds, requiring that all shooting take place in northern Finland during the months of November through February.

"What is *our* slice?" Sheldon Vanderbilt asked.

"Slice is not exactly the word," the famous producer replied. "We can have it in either cubes, blocks, or floes."

Whereupon Farber got to work putting the Sparrow Nightingale package together—with a Luxembourg-Andorra combine of Middle European psychoanalysts, proctologists, and gynecologists seeking a haven for their Eurodollars. It was a *little* less smooth than velvet. Just as the papers were about to be signed, the dark-eyed writer-director started to become difficult. First she refused to rewrite her script, then she refused to take a physical, and finally she refused to change her name, which turned out to be Johnny Tomasino. Then, at long last, Sheldon Vanderbilt's wife caught him coventuring with the young actress.

"How long has *this* been going on?" she demanded.

"It's the New Hollywood," Sheldon Vanderbilt exclaimed.

"And this," Mrs. Vanderbilt said, raising a six-shooter out of *Stagecoach*, "is the *Old* Hollywood."

Harry Farber, old pro that he is, simply took off for the Cannes Film Festival, where you can bet your bottom dollar that in no time at all, he'll find himself a live backer again.

Ubiquity
Will Get You Nowhere

One of the real problems facing us in the world today, particularly if we are professionals in show business and communications, is how to see everything and hear everything when practically all of it is going on at the same time in different theaters or on different networks. I mean, we all have just so much time, and there are limits to human ingenuity when it comes to problem solving.

I went to a movie last night at the Avco Theater. It happened to be a movie I wanted to see very badly. Now, there was *another* movie I wanted to see very badly, too, at the *Crest* Theater, but it went on at the same time as the one at the Avco Theater, so I sent my oldest son to the Crest Theater *for* me. Meanwhile, my *youngest* son was seeing still another picture for me at the *Village* Theater.

Realizing that by going to the Avco Theater I'd be missing

the "ABC Movie of the Week" on television, I persuaded my wife to stay home and watch that for me on the twenty-five-inch Quasar. She confessed to me that she had actually hoped to see a special on *CBS* at the time, so I set up the Sony Betamax to tape her special for later viewing. At the same time, I set the timer on the RCA Selecta Vision that was hooked up to our twenty-one-inch Zenith to tape the opening two hours of a new NBC mini-series that *neither* of us wanted to miss. And because I expected an important telephone call while I and the whole family would be thusly occupied, and because I knew what the call would be *about*, and what my viewpoint would be, I prerecorded all my thoughts in the matter on my Code-A-Phone machine and set the machine to handle the incoming call all by itself.

The point I'm trying to make is this: You would think, in this day and age, in a country that has sent men to the moon and probes to Mars and Venus and Jupiter, you would think that *someone* by now would have been able to figure out how to make it *unnecessary* for me to have had to go out to the Avco Theater in order to see the picture that was playing there. As it was, I created considerable disorder in the theater because of the portable, battery-operated Panasonic television set I held in my lap in order to watch still another movie that was running on the Z channel of our local cable-television setup, to which I was electronically linked. I can't say watching two movies at the same time with only one pair of eyes is the best way to appreciate even one movie, much less two, but what can a person do in a country whose technology is lagging so lamentably behind its ability to keep the world peaceful, free of unrest, and safe for democracy?

I've got to tell you that I worked myself into such a lather over the scientific and technological inadequacies of our Western civilization that, midway through the third reel of the movie at the Avco (and somewhere in the *fourth* reel of the movie in my *lap*), I took my miniature hand-held two-meter FM amateur radio transceiver from my belt and very quietly (so as not to disturb the theater audience) called my friend Byron in Brentwood to discuss the situation with him.

Unfortunately, Byron, though on the air at the time, was on a different repeater frequency, which I was unable to access because I did not have, in *my* transceiver, the subaudible tone encoder that would hold his repeater *in* for me. Undaunted, even lighting a match against the darkness (which is against the law at the Avco), I punched out Byron's telephone number on the miniature touch-tone pad of my little hand-held, and got Byron on the landline. I told him how upset I was, and why, and he agreed with me a hundred percent that something should be done to get science and technology *moving* in this country. We tossed ideas back and forth with surprising vehemence, until someone sitting in front of me in the theater complained that I was disturbing him and would I please shut up.

I thought he meant that I was interfering with his enjoyment of the movie on the screen, until I noticed the hearing device in his right ear which was remotely connected to a Norelco cassette player in his lap. I leaned closer to his ear for a moment and quickly discovered that he was listening to a taped playback of the previous night's Dodgers-Reds baseball game (which, later on, as we walked up the aisle, he told me he had missed because he was on a New York-to-L.A. 747 at the time in order to see a film that was so bad it had been released only to Inflight Motion Pictures. I asked him why he had wanted to see it if it was that bad, and he said that he was one of the film critics on a big national weekly newsmagazine and would go to any lengths to find a really lousy picture to review. I believed him, I really did, but I think he was lying to me.)

The young woman he was with, whose beauty was in no

way enhanced by the Pioneer stereo headset that she wore over her otherwise attractive auburn coiffure, held on to her escort's left hand so ardently that I felt impelled to inquire of her whether she was always so demonstratively affectionate in public, and she thereupon explained to me that affection had nothing to do with it. Through hand contact, and slightly damp palms, she was using her gentleman friend as an *antenna* for the tiny GE transistor radio in the left earpiece of her Yves. St. Laurent eyeglass frames, tuned, ironically enough, to the Dodgers-*Phillies* game, the Reds having already left town after losing four straight.

To get back to my discussion with Byron about the archaic state of American know-how in science and communications, we really didn't accomplish very much conversationally, what with the two movies I was watching at the same time, and the radio contact Byron was maintaining at *his* end with some other fellows on the two-meter repeater, and what with all the shushing I was getting from the man listening to the previous night's Dodgers-Reds game while holding hands, antenna-wise, with the young lady who was watching the movie while alternately listening to her stereo headphones and to the earpiece of her Yves St. Laurent eyeglasses broadcasting the Dodgers-Phillies game in present time.

So I set the Cruise Control in my Seville and drove over to Byron's house after the movies ended, first stopping off at my home to make sure that the Sony Betamax, the RCA Selecta Vision, the Code-A-Phone, and my wife were still working properly, and also to pick up my Radio Shack computer and its CRT monitor screen. At Byron's house, where he was now comfortably settled at the keyboard of *his* computer, which was interfaced with his IBM Selectric typewriter and programmed not only to deal with our upcoming chat but also to type notes on the proceedings, I set up my own com-

puter keyboard and screen, interfaced it with a teletype machine which would rattle off the notes on *my* end of the
conversation and automatically transmit the words via CW
on the twenty-meter amateur radio band to any part of the
planet that cared to listen, and then we started to address
ourselves to the problem at hand, namely: the failure of
American technology to move into the twentieth century,
much less the twenty-first, first mixing ourselves a rather gi-
gantic succession of *stiff* magaritas with a flip of the
Osterizer.

"What is the problem before us?" Byron asked his
computer.

"Apparently," replied the computer, "you men feel that
there ought to be an easier way to see a movie than to have to
be someplace and sit down, or even stand up, and *look* at it."

I tapped out a comment to *my* computer. "Is that too
much to ask?"

Byron turned to *me* this time. "What would you have preferred? What is your idea of the perfect solution?"

"Simple," I said to Byron, ignoring both computers, the
IBM Selectric, and the teletype machine. "All of my videocassette recorders at home, *whatever* their make or model,
are capable of recording television programs with the television set turned *off* and the house *empty*. Why cannot I
experience a *movie*, why cannot *my brain*, *my mind*, *my
memory cells* record the picture without my being there in the
theater at all? We've got a space probe on its way out to
Saturn now, for crying out loud. What am I doing in the
Avco Theater sitting behind some idiot listening to last night's
Dodger game holding sweaty hands with a girl who's got
Barry Manilow on her head and *tonight's* Dodger game in
her left ear? Are we living in the Stone Age or something?
What is this country coming to? I mean, *when* is this country
coming to?"

Byron looked at me wide-eyed. "By God, I think you've got it. . . ."

"Nah, nah, I just bought that flick on half-inch VHS format for sixty-five bucks. You've got the lyrics all wrong. It's 'I think *she's* got it.'"

"I think you've got it!" Byron exclaimed. "You send a *probe* to the theater, like we sent a probe to photograph *Jupiter*, except *this* probe is going to take sound pictures of the *movie screen*. . . ."

"Wait a minute. You mean I actually have to go to the movie house and set this probe down in a seat?"

"No, no," Byron said. "You get one of your *sons* to do that *for* you. And then this probe sends back pictures of the *movie*. . . ."

"To where? Sends them where?"

"*Right . . . here*." And he slapped his hand down twice on my computer's memory bank for emphasis, almost breaking it. "The whole movie gets stored in the computer, *which you will have programmed in advance to start delivering the picture to you while you sleep*. . . ."

"While I sleep? Then how do I *get* it?"

"Through the electrodes that have been inserted into your brain, dummy."

"What electrodes?"

"The ones attached to the electroencephalograph interfaced with your computer."

"I like it, I like it," I said, then scowled. "But do I have to actually *be* there in my bed with all those *things* sticking in my brain?"

"Hell, no," Byron said. "You get your *wife* to do it *for* you, and she tells you about it in the morning."

"Fantastic," I said. "Fantastic. Do you realize what we've come up with here tonight? Do you realize that this is *history* in the *making?* I'll never have to go to another movie in my whole life!"

Byron grinned with pleasure. "Pour me another margarita, huh?"

"But you've already had twenty-three," I said.

"Who's counting?" he said, frowning.

"*I* am," my computer replied.

And with one mighty swipe of his powerful drinking arm, Byron brought his fist down and smashed the delicate mechanism to bits.

Tomorrow night, I'm going to see *Poltergeist* at the Cinerama Dome.

If I Say So Myself . . .

Now and then I give seminars in screenwriting at two of the best-known cinema schools in Southern California. I do this mainly to pass on to young film students the priceless knowledge I have gained during my years in Hollywood. Actually, the knowledge isn't exactly *priceless*. My accountant can tell you, to the *dime*, how much it cost the studios for me to acquire this knowledge (before agents' commissions, Writers Guild dues, accountants' fees, legal expenses, psychotherapy, and federal and state income taxes).

The seminars usually unfold according to a series of set patterns. At the larger of the two schools, we screen one of my pictures, and afterward, the students raise their hands in turn and tell me what was wrong with the movie. Then I tell them what *I* think was wrong with the movie, and then I take the next hour or two, while holding their attention with savage personal anecdotes, to explain to them in detail how the producer first, the director second, the actors third, and the producer *again*, messed around with my screenplay and ruined the picture.

At the *smaller* school (and don't ask me why), things seem to go slightly differently. First I screen one of my films, and then the students take turns telling me how *terrific* it was, and which scenes they liked best, and why they liked them, and what a great screenplay I had written, and then I tell them how terrific *I* think the movie was, and why, and spend the next hour or two explaining how the producer, director, and the actors tried their very best to foul up my screenplay and destroy the picture, but failed.

It must now be obvious, from the above, that at all of my seminars, whether at the larger cinema school or at the smaller one, I am dedicated to getting across only one simple truth about the making of movies: There are no bad screenplays, only good and bad pictures.

What is disappointing to me is the number of my students at both schools who seem far more interested in "how to get into the business" than they are in learning anything about writing. Forget about concealing exposition, developing conflict, saying it with action instead of dialogue. How do I get myself an agent? How do I get a chance to direct? How do I get to be the head of a studio? Is there a cheaper way of taking over a movie company than making a tender offer? I keep telling them that their best chance to break into the world of motion pictures, whatever their ultimate goal, is to write a screenplay that is bought and produced and becomes a successful film. After that, they will be more than halfway home.

I don't know why they don't believe me. Or, if they don't actually disbelieve me, why they get restless and impatient, and find their way back to the same old questions: How can I get to be George Lucas, or Francis Coppola, or Martin Scorsese? Not *overnight. Today.*

Again I say, the entrée into the film industry is through *good writing*. It is the quickest way, the surest way, for me the *only* way. I say "for me," because perhaps *my* experience is the best case in point. And I've never ever revealed it before, not to my students or to anyone else. Call it modesty, call it discretion, call it *shame*, call it whatever you want, here it is, the hithero well-kept secret of how good writing catapulted *me* into the movie industry a long time ago.

I was a native New Yorker, living in the heart of Manhattan, dreaming of Hollywood, and barely making a living as a struggling writer of short stories and novelettes for the national magazines. By struggling writer I mean, I'd be sitting at my typewriter, with one hand trying to finish a story that was destined to be published in *Esquire*, or *Collier's*, or *Redbook*, while with the other hand I'd be struggling with a guy wearing a sheriff's uniform who was trying to yank me out of my desk because of a paltry few thousand dollars' worth of unpaid bills at Lord & Taylor, Saks Fifth Avenue, and Gristede Foods.

Hiding out in a $17-a-week room at the Hotel Paris in the West Nineties, I managed to complete a lengthy novelette called *Sweet Smell of Success*, about, among other things, a powerful Broadway columnist and the wicked, toadying press agent who served him well and lived off his crumblike favors. *Cosmopolitan* magazine bought it, and published it under another title, because the then editor, Herbert R. Mayes, didn't want the word "smell" in his magazine. (It wasn't until we did the film version seven years later, and the novelette was published as a book, that my original title came to life.)

Sweet Smell wasn't a bad piece of writing, not bad at all, if I say so myself, and I rarely do. Trouble was, a lot of Broadwayites jumped to the conclusion that my fictional columnist was meant to be Walter Winchell, and if that was Winchell, wasn't the press agent inevitably my close friend and former employer, the celebrated public-relations man, raconteur, wit, and New York–based daily columnist for the *Hollywood Reporter*, the late Irving Hoffman?

I had toiled as a writer of publicity material in Irving's swank Park Avenue offices for three years, and I had written much of the material that appeared in his daily "Tales of Hoffman" column in the *Reporter*. Even after I had left Irving's employ (to struggle with the sheriff), Irving had regularly sent me bulging envelopes of raw material with a friendly request to "see if you can jazz this stuff up for the column." I hadn't known how to say no, *Esquire* or no *Esquire*, sheriff or no sheriff.

And so, out comes my novelette on the newsstands, and in comes the phone call from Irving Hoffman summoning me to a tense confrontation in his apartment.

"How could you have *done* a thing like this to me? How *could* you?"

"Irving, it's only fiction. I'm a *writer*. And a writer can only write about the world he *knows*."

"Tell me the truth, *what did I ever do to you?*"

"You made me write those goddamn paragraphs for the *Reporter* when all I *had* was *time*, and what was left of my *brain*, to try to write short stories."

He didn't talk to me for more than a year. I was deader than Kelcey's. And it was nervous time around Broadway. Press agents would get up from the table at Lindy's if they saw me approaching. But not Sid Garfield. Sid Garfield was, and still is, one of the cleverest, most effective, and most popular publicity men in all of New York. Unfortunately for him at the time, he happened to have two close friends—Irving Hoffman and Ernest Lehman. The strain of my falling out with Irving pained Sid greatly. He didn't know what to say or not to say about me when he was with Irving, and the same about Irving when he was with *me*. It was embarrassing. It was unbearable. For all three of us.

I consoled myself during the year of terrible silence by renting the same room at the Hotel Paris and writing another novelette, this one called *The Comedian*. And when it was published in *Cosmopolitan* (before it later became a book, and an Emmy-winning "Playhouse 90" thanks to Rod Serling's brilliant dramatization), there was much excitement around New York, because the novelette was kind of well written, it kind of really was, if I say so myself, and I kind of tend to do that, I'm beginning to see.

Sid Garfield came to me, in an unusually cheerful mood. "I've been talking to Irving," he said. "I think he'd like to make up with you. He read *The Comedian* and asked me to ask you if you'd like him to say something about it in the *Reporter*."

"Gee, that's wonderful," I said. "Like what?"

"I don't know. I'll ask him," Sid said.

The next morning he phoned me. "Irving says, whatever you want. Just write him a short paragraph, and he'll run it."

A few days later, there appeared in the *Hollywood Reporter*'s "Tales of Hoffman" by Irving Hoffman an *entire column* devoted to nothing but praise for *The Comedian* and especially for its author. It began with a flourish: "This is going to be a plug. If you don't like to park in front of a plug, better move on right now. This is also going to be a suggestion to picture people. Any fool, including this one, can make suggestions. The wise man is the man who recognizes a good suggestion when it steps right out of the printed page and bites him on the kisser." On and on and on, in the most extravagantly glowing prose, right up to its glorious ending: "If some producer doesn't see to it that this guy covers his Broadway pallor with a Hollywood suntan, and soon, it will only prove that some people don't know a bite in the kisser when it steps right out of the printed page."

A week later, there we were—my wife and I and an infant son and a French poodle named Muffin—Hollywood-bound on the *Twentieth Century Limited* and the *Super Chief*, summoned to California by Paramount Pictures on a long-term screenwriting contract. They dropped Muffin's option after six months, but the rest of us are still here, and I like to think that it never would have come about had it not been for some *very* good writing.

Certainly *Sweet Smell of Success.*

Obviously *The Comedian.*

But let's not forget that column in the *Hollywood Reporter* —not one short paragraph but eight long ones—all of them beautifully written, if I say so myself, and I really do.

Reflections in a
Golden Garbage Can

You're a miserable, fickle bunch, all of you. You'll take a guy and set him up on a pedestal he never asked for. You'll make him your pet, your darling, your favorite of favorites. You'll read philosophic insights into his every one-liner. You'll fall down at his straight lines. For you, he is strictly can-do-no-wrong. And there's the rub.

You won't *let* him do wrong. You make him the prisoner of your adoration. He has to come through every time, or else. He has to *top* himself every time, or else. He is absolutely and positively forbidden to disappoint. Each time he goes to bat, a home run is not only expected, it is demanded. He *owes* it to you. Anything less than a home run is unforgivable. As for *striking out?* The death sentence.

You *know* who I'm talking about, of course. You *saw* "Reflections in a Golden Garbage Can." Obviously you did or you wouldn't be heaping such abuse on me. (Yes, *me*, getting *me* all confused in your mind with *him*.) You wouldn't have persuaded McDonald's not to let me play my kazoo there anymore on Friday nights. Shallow, vicious ingrates, that's what you are. I write *one* ill-conceived, self-centered mishmash of a piece called "Reflections in a Golden Garbage Can" and you *turn* on me as though I had written the sequel to *Mein Kampf*.

Why couldn't you have just tossed the pages across the room with a contemptuous exclamation like "yech" or "pheh" or "ich," or simply said, "OK, so he finally fell on his face, he's got a *right* to, maybe he felt he could *improve* it by falling on it?" But no, not *you*. That would have been too accepting, too humane, too forgiving. Instead, I'm "pretentious," I'm "narcissistic," I'm "egotistical," I'm "*not funny anymore*," I'm "*taking myself seriously*," I'm "*filled with self-hatred*," the typewriter has turned "*ugly*," I have "*loathing for my readers*," something has got to be "*done*" about me, I've "*gotten out of hand*," who do I think I am, "*Buchwald*, Russell *Baker*, Goodie *Ace*, Erma *Bombeck*, *La Roche-foucauld*?"

Where is it written into my contract with this universe that I'm not allowed to write *one bad piece*, that I'm not allowed *ever* to say that there must be more meaning to life than the creating of clever, witty, entertaining, satiric, biting essays on the movie business, that I cannot *ever* portray all of you as *fools* for reading me and taking me seriously and heaping adulation on me and clawing at me in the streets and begging me for my autograph and constantly, *forever*, interrupting every conversation I have with a woman, every wet kiss, every mad pass that I make, every physical assault that is made on *me* by every secretary and typist and Xerox operator and U.S. Mail clerk I come into contact with? If that happens to be "*the way it is*" in my life, why can't I *say so* without all this vitriol and viciousness directed at me? (Yes, *me*, the victim of your confusion of identities.)

Think of *this* possibility for a moment: You got so damn uptight, all of you, the minute you sensed that "Reflections" wasn't going to be the same old comfortable yuk-yuk thing, you didn't even stop to consider that maybe *I* wasn't being as serious about myself and my feelings and my life and my work as *you* were. You never stopped to consider that maybe it was all a *device* in which I was *pretending* that this was why I had turned out to be the me you all *think* you know and love (hate, as it turns out). Do you think, for one *minute*, that I actually *believe* all eyeglass frames make everyone look ugly, merely because I say so? Do you think, for one *second*, that because I tell you my brothers were ugly and my mother was ugly (which she wasn't, she was beautiful, but my brothers were not only ugly, they were *disgusting*), do you think that merely because I was writing this in what was clearly a fantasy, that it was necessarily a summation, a statement, an *excuse* for the fact that my *own* eyeglasses are ill-fitting?

After all the autobiographical fiction I've given you without one iota of complaint from you, suddenly I'm accused of having done a goddamn *documentary*, and what really, *really* bothers you is the way you see *yourselves* being "portrayed." "Egotistic," huh? Who's calling whom "narcissistic"?

Documentary? Come on, for crying out loud. If I say my secretary wormed her way out of typing a piece for me by pretending that she had herpes simplex and didn't want to spread anything around on the keys of her IBM Selectric, does that mean I deal in real life only with switch-hitting stenographers? Or could it be possible that I merely thought herpes simplex was somehow fresher and funnier than syphilis or psoriasis (which it isn't, *believe* me)? If you're going to *look* for significances, you're going to find them in everything. For example, my sitting at the card table on the beach, typing the piece with the pages blowing into the ocean—that must have been my way of saying, "Why couldn't I have authored *Gone With the Wind?*" Right? *Wrong.* I was merely trying to keep alive the suntan that hides the *real* tinsel underneath.

What about those white spaces, you say, where there were no words, no nothing, just blank pages? Uh-*huh.* He's trying to be Potluck Godard, Antonionioni, Federico Felipe. Right? *Nonsense.* The Correcto-Cartridge in my typewriter went haywire and overcorrected, that's all, and some of the editors around here are as metaphor-minded as you are, or they would have phoned me at my analyst's office (in the live crater of Mount St. Helens) and asked me for the missing words.

And while we're at it, just to make it official, I'd like to go on record as saying that the screenwriters' seminar at Lake Arrowhead *never took place.* True, I've given seminars. True, there have been retrospectives of films I have written. But this one, at the Garbage Can, was *pure invention.* I thought it would amuse you to hear film students saying those terrible, unthinkable, hostile remarks to my face, because that's the way film students really are. It isn't until much later, after they have graduated from school into the world of filmmaking, that they learn to do it behind your back. But apparently you were not amused. Not realizing that I was dealing in fantasy, you felt that I was sneering at your own admiration for me. You felt betrayed, slapped in the face.

Maybe it'll teach you a lesson. He who lives by the overpraise, dies by the overpraise.

Now let's talk for a moment about your hysterical accusations that I deliberately made my existence seem to be filled with monstrous, physically repellent people (one of you went so far as to say that I was the kind of writer who would have sent the crippled Philip in *Of Human Bondage* to an orthopedic surgeon who would have turned out to be "The Hunchback of Notre Dame." The *irony* of that remark is that I *believe* it was made by the author of *Nightmare Alley*. He's a fine one to talk).

The *fact* of my life is that, with a few exceptions, I am not exactly *surrounded, hemmed in,* by the Beautiful People. My gofer, for example, *actually had the role,* was about to be signed, without makeup, just before they decided to throw a piece of cloth over John Hurt and let *him* be *The Elephant Man*. And the neighborhood stationery store where I buy all my typing paper and ribbons and yellow pads (The Broken Pencil) happens to be managed by a woman who does all her seeing with her right eye, which is in a bag strapped to her right hip. But do I have to go on and on just to prove to you that not everyone in my life once had a singing acquaintance with Bert Parks? I think I've made my point. Ugliness is in the sty of the beholder.

OK, what's past is past. The question now is, what am I going to have to promise you—promise to do and not do—in order to get you to let me make a comeback, in order to be reasonably sure that you won't toss me aside to read the evening paper? You've still got blood in your eye. I can see that. You're still not all that inclined to forgive me. But I can't just lie down, I've gotta try *something*.

Tell you what I'm willing to do.

I'll never again pretend that there's anything neurotic or unpleasant or humiliating or vicious or degrading about the making of motion pictures, particularly with reference to what happens to writers and directors. I'll never again caricature film critics as glib, arrogant, self-promoting, parasitic show-offs, eager to ride coattails and broom handles to superstardom. I'll never again slander film buffs and cinema students and movie fans as weirdos who'll take either your autograph or your life.

More than that . . .

No more beach scenes, OK?

No more blank white spaces, OK?

No more openmouthed kissing, OK?

No more horn-rimmed glasses, only contacts, OK?

No more pimples or bad teeth or funny hairdos or misshapen bodies, OK?

No more *doing* before *thinking*, OK?

No more existential one-liners with the laugh at the end *missing*, OK?

No more time-and-place-and-narrative disorientation, OK?

No more structureless *mess*, OK?

No more talk talk talk talk talk talk, OK?

No more posturing as a sex object for schizoids, OK?

Oh yeah, and no more sick analysts, sick fathers, sick mothers, sick sisters, sick teachers, sick *little* me, and sick *big* me either, OK?

Now can I have my kazoo back?

Wait a minute! Who am I talking about? *I* didn't do anything!

"Hooray for Hollllywood . . . !"

Well, you won't have Lehman to kick you around anymore.

This is a piece saying farewell to the whole enchilada.

Parting is not such sweet sorrow either, don't let anyone kid you. There's nothing sweet about it at all. If typewriters had feelings, my Royal Standard would have tears in its *I*'s.

The truth is, I've run out of film folk to offend. It's time to move on. From now on, you're going to have to do your own offending. You're not going to get any more help from *me*. Go lose your *own* friends, go do your *own* antagonizing. I've probably alienated so many movie people I'll have to become an alien myself.

Watch out, Sigourney, I'm coming aboard.

I find it hard to believe that I've hung in this far. I can still remember the day I was invited to begin. Two weeks later, there it was, my first piece, returned to me by the publisher as unprintable.

I must have said something nice about someone.

Maybe this would be a good time for me to do it again. So I'll say it about you. You've been a perfect audience. You've been loyal, you've been understanding, you've been patient, you've been attentive, and you've made me very happy. The pleasure has really been mine. I really hate running out on you like this. I'll miss you much.

Because you've been paying attention, you already know how I came to be a member of the film community. What you don't know is that for many years thereafter, I ducked and flinched and feinted as I moved through the studio corridors, through the pathways of the jungle, waiting for all those awful people to spring out at me who I had been warned were there, and for all those terrible things to happen that were supposed to happen to you in Hollywood, especially if you came to it from New York, especially if you listened to the tales about it in New York. But nothing happened. I searched in vain for the monsters. I warded off blows that weren't there. It was quite disappointing.

Almost as disappointing as discovering that the Hollywood Party didn't exist either. I'm still looking for one. So are all my friends. We keep tripping over each other at sedate, refined, orderly, respectable, fully clothed, thoroughly enjoyable dinner parties, always asking each other, "Have you found one yet?" "Nope, have you?" "Twenty years now, but I'm not going to give up. There *must* be one out there somewhere."

I'm beginning to wonder.

Like a child who fantasizes imaginary friends to make up for the friends who aren't there, I seized the opportunity, when I began to fill up these pages, to create the Hollywood I felt *should* have been there. All screenwriters in these dream-like essays have been underpaid, unrecognized, mistreated, maligned, and totally helpless artists. All directors have been self-aggrandizing egomaniacs. All producers have had only one slogan: "The buck stops here please." All studio executives have been migrant workers. All male superstars have been preshrunk. Envy, jealousy, greed, and covert hostility have been the Four Horsemen of the Apocalypse Now. Youth is so wonderful, what a shame to waste it on young directors. Hollywood children start their prayers: "Our Father who art in Heaven's Gate . . ."

I wish I could say it was a world I never made, but I can't, because I did make it, on paper anyway. And perhaps I've been convincing here and there. Maybe some of you have been buying the dream and taking it for reality, particularly you young film students. Of such stuff as this are vicious cycles perpetuated. From the cinema schools of the nation they pour forth, the fresh-eyed young men and women, onto the sound stages of filmland, expecting to experience the fictional reality of rejection and humiliation, and not finding it, *create* it anew out of their own soap bubbles, to assuage their confusion at being warmly welcomed, respected, and given the ball to run with as they see fit.

Should they fail as filmmakers, at least they'll know who and what to point the finger at.

Someday, someone may figure out how to write about "the movie business" as it really is without being hooted at and reviled and disbelieved. But such a person could wind up as a latter-day Joe or Joan of Arc. Such a person would be a threat to almost every writer about film in the world, for it is apparently as important as a belief in God that we be permitted to believe in a Hollywood of corruption, mediocrity, stupidity, and venality. The yearly miracles of movies that turn out well fail to sway the multitudes, who cling to their faith, who *must* believe that Hollywood can do no right.

They are so wrong.

At the risk of being reviled (which is no risk at all, because you won't be able to *find* me, and what the heck do *I* know anyway), I will now tell you what I have long believed to be true, and have just as long been reluctant to acknowledge. The film community of California, hereinabove referred to as Hollywood, is a community of serious-minded, industrious, highly skilled specialists—artists, craftspersons, technicians, executives, supervisors—interested to the point of obsession almost exclusively in their work, proud of their accomplishments, miserable over their failures, consumed by the demands of their occupations, striving endlessly for elusive excellence, dreaming constantly of artistic and commercial success, reluctantly taking bits and pieces of time off to play, but mainly eating work, sleeping work, talking work, thinking work, working work, forever getting up off an infinity of floors after numberless counts of ten, walking into unending storms of rights and lefts to the chin and to the heart as well, taking the jeers of the critics when they deserve it and the indifference of the public when they've earned it, coming back, coming back, coming back, always coming back, wanting another chance, maybe this time they'll get it right, refusing to face the possibility that they really don't know how, anything to keep getting the chance to try it again, angrily brushing off ill health and onrushing time, cursing anything that gets in the way of their determination to keep on doing whatever it is that they've learned how to do and to do it well and have it noticed and admired and rewarded and applauded, and the amazing thing is that out of all this striving and struggle there comes a great boon to the world, comes pleasure, comes entertainment, comes laughter and tears and illumination and knowledge and identification and understanding and relief from care for all the people in the world who need it in their lives, which is everyone, just about everyone, and these hardworking members of the film community of California, who occasionally do something right, who now and then see a fragment of their dream come true, who see a marvelous movie magically come forth from their efforts, some of them do, once or twice in their lifetimes, the fortunate ones do, which is why there are a hundred films or so that no one alive will ever forget, out of the thousands that have been made, these foolish, touching, single-minded dreamers who spend the best and the worst years of their lives putting all this effort into trying to get something good up on a movie screen, will take all the ridicule and contempt and derision you can throw at them because they know that it comes with the territory, which is known as Hollywood, just as an Alaskan will take snow in winter if he wants to be an Alaskan, and nothing will stop the people of Hollywood, certainly not the snow in winter, certainly not you with your scorn and your sniping and your condescension from afar, you'll never stop them, nor you with your patronizing pronouncements from the Olympian heights of your subway trains, you'll never stop them, they'll just keep on coming back for more, and coming back and coming back, and not even death will stop them, because right behind them are all the others waiting for a chance to have a go, who'll take all the misery and pain and punishment you can inflict on them as long as they can continue to fight and struggle to get back up again and try to do something well, to get something right, even though they know that it's just about impossible to do, that a good picture is a miracle that almost never happens, but that's not going to stop them, *nothing* is going to stop them, but go ahead, keep trying, like you've been trying for years, and don't let defeat get you down, just as *they* don't let defeat get *them* down. But have some fun now and then, will you? Don't take the effort so seriously. Relax, laugh a little, enjoy yourselves.

See you at the movies. Okay?